ESSEX
VILLAINS

W.H.JOHNSON

COUNTRYSIDE BOOKS
NEWBURY, BERKSHIRE

COUNTRYSIDE BOOKS
3 Catherine Road
Newbury, Berkshire

To view our complete range of books,
please visit us at
www.countrysidebooks.co.uk

ISBN 1 85306 882 9

Designed by Peter Davies, Nautilus Design
Produced through MRM Associates Ltd., Reading
Typeset by Mac Style Ltd, Scarborough, N. Yorkshire
Printed by J.W. Arrowsmith Ltd., Bristol

Contents

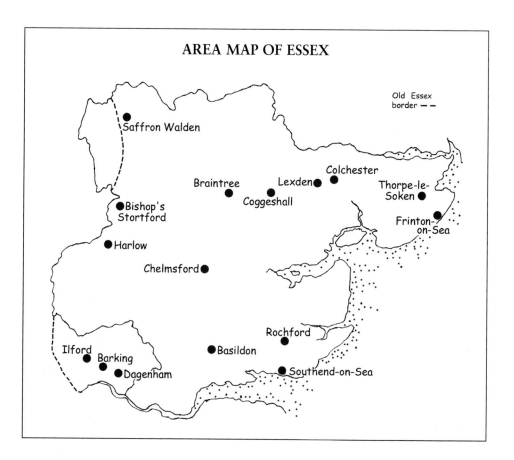

AREA MAP OF ESSEX

Old Essex border − −

Saffron Walden

Braintree

Lexden

Colchester

Thorpe-le-Soken

Coggeshall

Frinton-on-Sea

Bishop's Stortford

Harlow

Chelmsford

Rochford

Ilford

Barking

Basildon

Dagenham

Southend-on-Sea

INTRODUCTION

───────────❀───────────

Now here's a gallery of villains to match any in the land. I have tried to vary their activities so that among them there are stick-up men and kidnappers, drugs barons and fearsome racist thugs, a would-be spy, a trio of fraudsters, a serial-killer and a bent solicitor. Because I have restricted myself to the past 30 years or so, many of the cases included here have not previously appeared in book form.

Perhaps having presented some members of the cast, I ought to explain what I mean by the words 'villain' and 'villainy'. There are most certainly degrees and types of both which I hope will be apparent in these pages. A couple of the characters led more or less blameless lives until their one offence recorded here. Then, of course, there are the professional villains, those who acknowledge that the chance of being caught is a natural hazard of their lives. And at the furthest extreme there are those distorted souls whose gross offences place them within the deepest circles of depravity and wickedness. Having confined myself to the years after 1970, you will meet no sepia-tinted old criminals here, no henpecked husbands ultimately driven to violence, no lavender-scented old ladies handy with the poison bottle. The characters in this book are, for the most part, more robust than that. Some are larger than life and seem to fairly leap off the page. Some you might even imagine as agreeable social companions in certain social contexts though in truth you could never bank on that.

Not all of the villains in this book have lived in Essex. Several simply came visiting, did their dirty work, and went back to their homes, in some cases leaving behind them their desperately damaged victims. But others were – are, in fact – most definitely in and of the county.

There will be readers who do not recognise the Essex described here. But it is a fact that a large percentage of the country's most dangerous and organised criminals live in the county. Think first of its proximity to the East End of London and then of its miles of unguarded coastline, ideal for landing goods from the Continent. Mercifully, the greater part of the county is undamaged, undeniably beautiful, and safe for the great majority of its residents.

May I at this point thank Mrs Susan Bishop for agreeing to the inclusion of the account of the murder of her gallant husband.

Any errors in the interpretation of the facts in this book are wholly mine. To any whose copyright I have failed to acknowledge, I apologise. Any omissions will be corrected in the next printing.

In conclusion, I hope that readers will find *Essex Villains* entertaining and interesting.

W. H. Johnson

WHO WANTS TO BE A MILLIONAIRE?

— ❁ —

Peter Boardman, the Leigh solicitor, must have wondered about his client even though he had acted for her for the last ten years. But then, there is no end to the odd ways in which people behave. Years earlier Annie Kay had inherited a considerable sum of money from her father, a dentist, who had invested his money very wisely. And she in turn had made wise investments so that now, at the age of 87, she was a millionairess – though no one would have guessed it – holed up in the Spillman's three-bedroom semi in Guildford Road in Southend rather than in the top-class nursing home she most certainly could have afforded. There again, the solicitor probably told himself, she had never been one for the extravagant life.

Odd, too, that in recent years she, a naturally reserved woman who had never married, had teamed up with Patrick Wedd, a perfectly respectable man she had met on holiday. He had gone to live with her in her semi-detached Dawlish Drive bungalow in Leigh, and there is no doubt about their mutual devotion. Wedd had a flat in Folkestone and the couple used to spend their summers there and sometimes they would take a foreign holiday. Not that these jaunts ever ate significantly into her funds.

A well-meaning woman, Miss Kay had decided to leave the bulk of her fortune to charity. Over the years she had frequently visited the Southend-on-Sea Home for the Blind, as the highly accomplished pianist of a local concert party. And she had also admired Scope – formerly the Spastics Society – which does so much for the disabled, both adults and children. Both of these organisations were to receive major bequests in her will. All these good intentions, all these sincere wishes to help the unfortunate, while Miss Kay and Wedd, growing older, were less and less able to look after themselves. She now weighed 16 stone and walked with the aid of a Zimmer frame. Her modest bungalow was a squalid wreck, neglected, dirty and unhygienic. It was infested with flies and ants in the summer and at all times there was an unpleasant smell about the place. The community care nurse who used to visit Miss Kay to attend to her ulcerated legs said that it was not the sort of place that anyone would want to spend much time in.

It seemed the right idea, then, in July 1996, for the two old people to decide to leave the bungalow and go to live with the Spillmans. After all, they knew 47-year-old Annette Spillman who for some months had been their home-help and who had had experience of running her own care home. They had implicit trust in Annette and it has been said that at this time Miss Kay was so fond of her that she thought of her as her daughter.

Southend-on-Sea Home for the Blind. (Robert Hallmann)

In January 1997 Patrick Wedd died, leaving Annie £180,000. When, within days, Peter Boardman called to discuss the new provisions to her will, the old lady was adamant that the bequests that she had already drawn up should stand but that the will should now be redrafted.

On this occasion she said she wanted to leave donations to the Children's Society – Wedd's favourite charity – as well as to Scope and to the Southend Home for the Blind.

Boardman went off to draw up the revised document, unaware that he would never see Miss Kay again. When he telephoned her a week or so later to tell her that all was ready for signing, it was Annette Spillman who took his call. Miss Kay had been dissatisfied with his service, he was told. She had put her affairs in the hands of another local solicitor. Such a snub was undoubtedly personally hurtful to the solicitor but people often have to shrug their shoulders at slights of this nature. They just have to get on with their work and their lives. It wasn't like Miss Kay, quite out of character really, to behave in this manner but, as Boardman knew well enough, old people sometimes do make seemingly irrational decisions. But even so, Boardman had suspicions. He had not cared for Mrs Spillman when he had called at Guildford Road to speak to Miss Kay about the will. She had kept coming into the room where he and Miss Kay were talking and had finally sat down without invitation at the table. But the intrusion had apparently not disturbed his client, and so he had not felt able to raise an objection. Furthermore, Boardman was of the view that the old lady was no longer especially satisfied with her situation at the Spillmans and was considering a move.

Then, in March 1997, within weeks of Miss Kay's break with her solicitor, she died. And some days later Peter Boardman learnt that she had made a new will with another firm only eight days before her death and that she had left significant bequests to Annette and David Spillman. He was distinctly uneasy – uneasy enough to contact a former Essex Detective Sergeant, Roy Cook. Spillman? David Spillman? Cook knew him well enough; he had come across him a few times. Petty stuff but all the same David Spillman was one to be watched, the solicitor was told.

Now Boardman, thoroughly alerted, got in touch with Scope, the charity due to benefit by £1,000,000, half of what Miss Kay had left. But Scope, it turned out, had not heard about any bequest from Miss Kay. Their legacy co-ordinator, Paul Martin, instantly obtained a caveat on the will which enabled him to freeze the money. He then put investigation of the matter in the hands of yet another lawyer, Peter Jeffreys. An enthusiastic reader of Dorothy L Sayers, this was just up Jeffreys' street. For him, this investigation had all the elements of a first-class thriller.

Jeffreys obtained copies of both the old and new wills. The latter left most of Miss Kay's cash to the Spillmans – 'my good friends', she called them – with £10,000 for 'my dear friend Annette Russill'. Enlisting the help of a private investigator, Jeffreys tracked down Annie Kay's few close friends and neighbours, none of whom had ever heard of Mrs Russill. 'At this stage,' Jeffreys said, 'I thought the new will had been made under influence. Yet, according to the solicitor's note of the meeting, I knew Annette and David Spillman had not been there when it was signed.'

This was puzzling. Why were the Spillmans not present when the will was signed? It was then that Jeffreys realised that the second will had been signed in February 1997 at Dawlish Drive where Miss Kay had not lived since moving in with the Spillmans in July 1996. 'I knew the will was signed at Dawlish Drive,' Jeffreys said, 'so, if Miss Kay had not been there, someone else must have signed it.' And a handwriting expert who compared the new will with cheques known to have been signed by Miss Kay concluded that it was unlikely that she had signed the second will.

So who did sign the will? Jeffreys had little doubt. 'I thought if Russill had suddenly rocketed into the frame, she must be the person who had signed the will, and the £10,000 was her cut. Everything fitted perfectly,' he said. But if the theory was sound, he was unsure quite how to prove it. At this point he called in the police.

When Detective Superintendent David Bright of the Essex Police Fraud Squad began to investigate the concerns of Boardman, Martin, and Jeffreys, he recognised that the old people might not have died from natural causes. Before dawn on 17th

July 1998, in the presence of police officers and a Home Office pathologist, the bodies were exhumed at the Sutton Road cemetery in Southend. On the same day a post-mortem was carried out. Whilst evidence of sedative drugs was found, it was immediately acknowledged by the police that it would not be possible to prove who had administered them nor would it now be possible to estimate what effect the drugs had had. That particular line of enquiry was abandoned. Nevertheless, later that day, Annette and David Spillman and Annette Russill, the stepmother of Annette Spillman, were arrested and charged with conspiracy to defraud.

At first Annette Spillman claimed that there had been no attempt to deceive Annie Kay. In a statement to her solicitor, she explained how Miss Kay and Patrick Wedd had come to stay in July 1996. 'It became clear they could not care for each other in

Sutton Road cemetery where Patrick Wedd and Annie Kay were buried. (Robert Hallmann)

the bungalow,' Annette Spillman said. 'Both had their marbles despite their physical difficulties. Our concern was to treat them kindly and help them live in a decent way for as long as they could.' But she rejected the suggestion that either she or her husband had ever tried to persuade the old woman to leave her money to them. Sometimes Miss Kay had told them that she had no-one to leave her money to, as she had no family. But Spillman said, 'David and I never picked up on these remarks. We were not interested. Another time she said, "I will leave you something in my will." I did not question her about this. I would not have done as she would have realised I was being manipulative.' She went on to say that she had had no idea that Miss Kay was so wealthy a woman until after her death. And she had her own version of Peter Boardman's visit to Guildford Road. She said that Miss Kay asked her to stay in the room, telling her that she was not sure she would hear everything the solicitor was saying. According to Annette Spillman, as Boardman talked to Miss Kay, the old woman kept looking across at her, pulling faces and winking. It was clear, Spillman said, that Boardman was trying to persuade her lodger to leave her money to charity and that Miss Kay was unwilling for this to happen. This was why she had changed her solicitor. This is why Mark Goodson, a legal clerk, had come to draw up the new will for Miss Kay.

But by the time of her trial Annette Spillman had changed her story and had admitted her part in the conspiracy. The older woman, Annette Russill, her stepmother, made no attempt to shield the other two. Almost immediately pleading guilty to conspiracy to defraud, she heavily implicated the Spillmans. From now she presented herself as a somewhat put-upon, rather defenceless woman. She had been bullied by David Spillman, who threatened to harm her, her boyfriend and her dog if she did not cooperate. She had been compelled to play her part, she said. It was David and Annette, her own daughter, who made her deceive Mark Goodson: it was they who forced her to practise Annie Kay's signature. The police had found an envelope from the Benefits Agency on which she had repeatedly written Miss Kay's signature. The others had coached her, telling her what they wanted her to do. It had been hard for her, she protested. She had never learnt to write and she had been forced under David Spillman's tutelage to practise the signature 'every spare moment', not that he had always been understanding of her difficulties. 'We're not asking you to shift mountains,' he'd said to her in irritation at her slowness in mastering the forgery. 'It's only a bloody signature we want you to do.'

'It is not my fault I cannot read or write,' she told the court. 'I am not a bad person.' Not that David Spillman saw her in that light. He claimed that 'Russill is probably the last person on earth I would trust with anything'. But then Spillman had decided to plead not guilty and to detach himself from both women.

At their trial at Basildon Crown Court in August 1999, the astonishing tale unravelled, a story of how three ill-educated people had tricked lawyers and bankers by redrafting the will and fraudulently drawing cash from the dead woman's account. Detective Superintendent David Bright who led Operation Fool's Gold, responded much as Jeffreys had. He too felt it was 'an amazing case', the most remarkable in all his years of service, more like fiction than real life, more the kind of case to be looked into by Wexford or Morse. This ingenious case, he said, 'had so many unusual features'. 'How often do you get a case where so many professional people are called as witnesses? It's not often you see barristers and solicitors in the witness box giving evidence.' The fraud, which in David Bright's words 'would have set up all three accused for life', had been planned over some months and was put into action when Patrick Wedd died in early 1997.

The plan was both ingenious and simple. Martyn Levett for the prosecution outlined the cunning the trio had employed. 'In order to get their hands on the money, the Spillmans and Russill had to follow a plan and each of the three played a part. They followed this agreed plan whereby they were going to deceive the will-maker, a firm of solicitors, and even a barrister.'

The Spillmans had realised that under their roof they housed two vulnerable elderly people whose combined money would make them rich. And how could anyone query what they were doing? If they just waited for Miss Kay's death, there would be no problems. She had only one relative living in Yorkshire. They thought they could easily deceive her. (They were mistaken. Margaret Collins, Annie Kay's cousin, contacted the Spillmans when her cousin did not write her usual newsy letters to her. She was told that Annie had died nine months earlier. Suspicious, she initiated her own enquiries, sending for copies of the death certificate and the will. She then discovered that the police were making enquiries.) As soon as Patrick Wedd died, the Spillmans rid themselves of Peter Boardman, employed a new solicitor who did not know the background, and started dipping into the old woman's funds. Using forged cheques signed by Annette Russill, they drew more than £25,000 from her bank and building society accounts. Russill, disguised as Annie Kay, cashed at least one cheque at the bank. As a reward for their efforts, the Spillmans were able to go on holiday with their ten-year-old son.

On three occasions in February 1997 Mark Goodson called at Miss Kay's bungalow in Dawlish Drive to go over changes to her will. On a fourth occasion he called to see his client at the Spillmans' home. The changes to the will were substantial but it was not Mark Goodson's brief to persuade Miss Kay not to make them. A few weeks later Goodson received a telephone call. It was Annette Spillman. 'We've lost Annie,' she told him. After expressing his condolences, Goodson asked when the funeral was to take place. Too late, she told him sadly, Annie Kay was already buried.

But that was the trick of it. That is how it was done. Mark Goodson never saw the real Annie Kay. He had been duped. He'd been dealing with a bogus client. When he went by arrangement to meet Miss Kay at Dawlish Road, he had no reason to believe the old woman in the wheelchair was other than a bona fide client. How could he have guessed the lengths that had been gone to in order to deceive him? Sixty-four-year-old Annette Russill had played the part of a woman more than 20 years her senior. And so, cut from the new will were the bequests to Scope, the Children's Society and Southend Blind Society. In their stead came the names of David and Annette Spillman and Miss Kay's alleged 'dear friend, Annette Russill'. They were to be rewarded for their 'loving care and kindness'.

Before Goodson's arrival at the bungalow, all photographs of Annie Kay were hidden. No need arousing suspicions. And then

Annette Spillman had to help her mother to dress in Miss Kay's clothes, to make a seven stone woman pass for one weighing more than twice as much. But let Annette Russill herself explain what happened.

'I had two black sweaters on, very thick, to fill me out a lot. Annette did my hair and my face in the hall. She had already taken over Annie's make-up and stuff and one of my wigs that looked a bit like Annie's. She put a lot of make-up on my face and blackened my eyes and put the wig on and put the hairnet over it. I didn't look quite right so then she asked me to remove my teeth, top and bottom, so it would look better.'

Annette Russill had been well rehearsed in what she had to say. The innocent Goodson, taken in as most people would have been, took instructions from his client, understanding the changes in her will to be out of her gratitude to the Spillmans who had been so kind to her. And the elder Annette awarded herself £15,000, too, before signing the will. It was out of this sum that she bought a sporty little Vauxhall Tigra. Once the will had been signed, all three set to and dusted and washed away all signs of their having ever been at the bungalow – water and Dettol, and not a fingerprint left.

Passing sentence, Judge Francis Petre said that the three had actively engaged in a fraud that was 'mean, devious, carefully planned and highly successful'.

David Spillman was jailed for seven years, and his wife, Annette, for five years and three months for conspiracy to defraud and 18 months on two theft charges, the sentences to be served concurrently. Annette Russill was given three years for conspiracy to defraud, three years for forgery, and 18 months for theft, the sentences to run concurrently.

Enough, though, of the villainy. What about the villains? What seems clear is that by the time the case came to court each of them detested the other two. Indeed, David Spillman's and Annette Russill's intense dislike of each other was of long standing.

At the time of the trial David Spillman and his wife had separated. He had just served five months in prison for causing her actual bodily harm. And this was not his first offence, as Roy Cook had told Peter Boardman. In the past he had had spells inside for theft and robbery. The Spillman marriage was turbulent, littered with frequent argument, threats and constant fallings-out. In recent years David Spillman's work record had been sporadic on account of his drinking. 'My doctor considers me a chronic alcoholic,' he admitted. In 1966 he had lost his driving licence and could no longer work as a long-distance lorry driver. Times were difficult and for three years Annette had been running their house as a care home but, unable to cope, she became a home-help. And it was then that she went to work at Miss Kay's bungalow in Dawlish Drive. This was when the first seeds of the plan germinated. And now was the time that Annette Russill came back into her daughter's life.

For years the two Annettes had had an uncertain relationship. Sometimes they resolved their differences and met frequently. At other times they were at loggerheads, rarely meeting without fierce disagreements. In 1996, for example, so cool were they towards each other that they did not meet at all. In the early months of the following year – remember that Patrick Wedd died in January 1997 and Annie Kay in March – they were again on close terms. But once the two women were in custody awaiting trial, special arrangements had to be taken to keep them apart until they came into the dock. Russill's defence counsel claimed that she was worried about being sent to Holloway where her daughter was being held.

Annette Russill had a somewhat racy and rackety background. In the 1980s she had cared for elderly people at her Rochford home. In a statement read to the court, one former neighbour, harking back to Russill's unregistered care home, said that on some occasions shouting and sobbing had been heard from the house. Her convictions for theft dated back to 1953. Barely literate but undoubtedly plausible, she had over the years drawn £10,000 from the DSS for a non-existent twin sister.

Paul Martin from Scope said, 'In my 40 years of probate experience, I have never come across a case like this before or one even remotely like it.' And certainly without him, the suspicious nose of Peter Boardman, former detective Roy Cook, and Peter Jeffreys, the Dorothy L Sayers fan, the scam might never have been uncovered. As for the Spillmans, their appeal to the High Court against the length of sentence failed in October 2000. And best of all, Miss Kay's bequests went to their rightful recipients.

THE CZAR OF
SOUTH-EAST ESSEX

There will be those who will say it is a slur but unquestionably the place has aroused strong feelings. Basildon, one of the new towns, is described in an *Observer* article in 1996 as 'a concrete crime against humanity, committed in the early 1960s as a Utopian act to free East Enders from the filth and depravity of London'. The great overspill has in part succeeded, bringing to the emigrants from London and to their children and grandchildren a distinct improvement in living standards. Better a tower block than a squalid run-down terrace house in a rat-run of alleyways; better a tedious estate than a derelict tenement; better the factory than the dole. But that is one side of the picture. There's comfortable living here, too, no matter what the man from the *Observer* says, and it has to be admitted that there is some first-class housing and little unemployment in this part of Essex. There's money to spend. There are pubs and clubs, new cars in the drive, and holidays to all parts of the world, just down the road from Stansted and Heathrow. So why complain about Basildon?

Is it because in recent years a deeper, more wasting depravity than ever has been detected? Is this why there are references to the 'Basildon Badlands'? And not just from some fancy journalist living in Highgate. The writer Bernard O'Mahoney described it as a violent town in the 1990s, 'where peroxide blondes, cheap drinks and drunken nights were commonplace'. Stereotyping it may be but O'Mahoney knows this place, its darkest side. He has been part of its destructive culture, part of the Essex drugs scene, not as a user but as a member of a powerful gangland distribution system. He has been a minder when major deals have taken place.

And he knows the clubs. He was one of Tony Tucker's doormen, working as the head of security at Raquel's where the student Leah Betts is alleged to have bought her fatal Ecstasy tablet. And he can vouch for the punishment beatings, the intimidation, and the ferocious responses that are part and parcel of the drugs trade.

The majority of the people living there, law-abiding, responsible folk, have long been concerned about the rotten, dangerous edge of life in Basildon. They hear of the overdoses, the gang fights, the gunshot wounds, the fatal stabbing of some petty offender only two or three years out of school. The local newspapers recount such tales with fearful regularity for their town is a magnet for dealers. It's not a huge place, Basildon, but there's room here for more than one big dealing gang. And the readers breathe a momentary sigh of satisfaction when they hear that another peddler has been apprehended and sentenced and yet reflect that one more gang broken merely leaves a vacancy for its successor.

Of course, the location of Essex is ideal for drugs distribution. The drugs are shipped in from the Continent into what is one of the principal gateways for trade. Here there are first-class links to London via the M25, the A13 and the A127. Light aircraft land at farms; inflatable boats with high-powered engines cross the Channel and slide by night into deserted creeks. The importation of drugs into south-east Essex is, to the outsider, on an unimaginable scale. It is colossal, and those at the top deal in millions of pounds. This is a serious business. Customs and police are hard-pressed to stop such a regular volume of trade.

In this world of high finance, business is conducted in the shadow of violence. In this reckless world on the edge of the capital, the executives carry guns, knives, baseball bats, ammonia; they own elegant residences, drive Rolls Royces and Range Rovers; their power-boats winter in foreign marinas; their children's ponies are stabled in the paddock.

But they sometimes fail, these ruthless men. Drugs barons are toppled and end their days inside or face long sentences. In 1992 Jason Lee Vella became a significant figure in the drugs world. In July 1995, a millionaire not yet 25, he was sent down for 17 years.

Vella, originally from East Tilbury, came early into the business after a period of market-stall trading with his Maltese father. He started drug dealing in his teens and from his earliest days as a dealer was determined to build his own drugs empire in Basildon. It's never easy to build an empire of any kind and in the world of drug trafficking it is especially difficult for there are rivals who resent anyone, let alone an upstart boy, moving in on the territory. But, by sheer force of will and an almost unparalleled use of violence, Jason Vella, 'a creepily handsome control freak', clambered in a short space of time to the top of his muckhill. Just as he had planned, he was on his way to the very top. Some were to say that he had already reached it, that his empire already rivalled that of his long-gone heroes, the Krays. There was never anyone to touch Ronnie and Reggie in Vella's eyes. He watched over and over again the video of the brothers' life story. They were his models, his never-to-be-forgotten heroes. There was neither irony nor disrespectful intent when he named his Vietnamese pot-bellied pigs Ronnie and Reggie, nor indeed when in a fit of pique he threw one of the animals out of a moving car on the M25. How it was that the second met its sudden end is not recorded.

The brothers would be proud of him, he must have thought. How could they not be? According to Simon Renoldi, who kept the gang's accounts, when he was not engaged in dealing in drugs or meting out violence, the gang's turnover, in less than a year, was £1.2 million.

Small wonder that Jason Vella drove a BMW and his girlfriend, a Golf; small wonder that he enjoyed frequent holidays to Tenerife and the United States, or that he was able to take six of his chums, all in their usual designer outfits, to the Lennox Lewis fight in Las Vegas and to pay £5,600 at the airport for their seats to be upgraded to club class. While in America, Vella hired a chopper to fly his boys around the Grand Canyon. He looked after his followers, provided they did as he expected. Nothing but the best for them. He was generous. He could afford to be. The trade gave him more money than he knew what to do with. The money flowed in because there was a massive market and he had the nerve to dip into it. Other gangs shared the Basildon pot of gold with him, each seemingly satisfied that, for the moment anyway, there was enough for everyone.

Vella bought Ecstasy from Dutch dealers and sold it on to street dealers. From them the tablets went across the social spectrum to the desperate unemployed and to the wealthy businessmen who worried that their own children might one day be approached at the school gates – as they were.

Basildon, now Vella's own town, was a ready market, where it was never possible to satisfy demand. So too was Tilbury, another of his bases. But he was selling further afield than that. His couriers went all over London and the Home Counties and way beyond – up to the north-west and to Scotland. It was no small business enterprise for it included a protection racket as a lucrative sideline and to ensure that he stayed on top, the opposition was ruthlessly sought out and brutally dealt with. Torture was the order of the day for anyone who crossed Jason Vella. The notoriety of his gang soon spread and no one in the area cared to challenge him. He was, as Mr Justice Simpson was to say, 'the Czar of south-east Essex'.

Although the police were aware of Vella's activities, they found it impossible to find enough evidence to bring him before the courts. The lengthy, complex and sometimes dangerous Operation Max, led by Detective Superintendent David Bright, was established to collect evidence about the gang's activities. But after two years the police were still frustrated because, although they possessed information about both his drug trafficking and the calculated violence which Vella employed against those who displeased him, they could find no witnesses to support the case they were seeking to bring. No one, it appeared, would trust the police to save them if they were to make a complaint against Vella. His reputation was too formidable. He traded in fear, confident that no one would ever dare speak out against him. So the trafficking went on; victims, beaten, scarred, and tortured, were found but none was ever courageous enough to point the finger at Jason Lee Vella. That is, until Reggie Nunn decided that he had had enough.

The Reggie Nunn incident gives a clear idea of Jason Vella's style of man-management. When his followers failed him they received the same treatment as the opposition. That Reggie Nunn did fail his leader is not in doubt. And the retribution was fierce.

On the evening of 30th July 1993, Nunn accompanied his boss to 65 Hollands Walk, Vella's rented house in Vange. He hoped he'd be able to make a clean breast of things. He'd let Jason down and he wanted to explain his failure, to tell him that he would rectify matters. He just needed a little time. He'd been silly and he knew that but he hoped that Jason would understand. But what Jason Vella understood was that the £7,000 that he'd been expecting from Reggie Nunn wasn't forthcoming. He'd given Reggie 1,000 Ecstasy tablets to take to Scotland. Each tab was worth between £10 and £15, and Reggie was expected to sell them for about £15,000. It had been agreed that they would share the proceeds. But Reggie Nunn had been thoughtless. He'd spent more than he should on expenses. He couldn't quite give Jason as much as he was expecting. In fact there was very little left. And Jason, along with another of his heavies, Scott Hunt, had had to chase off to Scotland to pick him up.

So, somewhat apprehensive, Reggie goes with Jason to the house in Hollands Walk. Is Jason angry with him, he wonders. The gang members, Reggie's pals, are present, half a dozen or more of them waiting in the first-floor sitting room, and they're aware of how the boss is going to respond. It's a kangaroo court. That's the way Jason deals with people who step out of line. And the gang will, as always, blindly follow his lead, adopt his viciousness. They will not question what he does, nor will they question their own actions as they join in the torture beating. His sadism has become their unthinking response to Reggie's folly. The boss will grossly humiliate him, just as he always does to whoever has upset him, and so will the young men sitting there, waiting for the victim. They will do what is expected of them.

'Why did you do it, Reggie?' Jason asks him. Reggie knows he's in trouble, knows it's going to be really bad for him. Jason is carrying an epee. He raises it over his head and brings it down, the narrow blade opening up Nunn's cheek.

'There's blood on my settee,' Jason complains, attacking Reggie again. Then the others join in, punching him to the floor and kicking him. Jason slashes him again and yet again. 'Stop whimpering like a little boy,' he shouts as Reggie cowers in an attempt to ward off the blows.

Hollands Walk where Reggie Nunn was tortured. (Robert Hallmann)

'You know it's not going to end here, Reg,' he hears Jason say. And then he hears something about keeping him here overnight and finishing him off in the morning. Reggie fears that this is no idle threat. He knows what 'finishing off' may mean. And the very thought of what may happen to him tomorrow, the knowledge that in the meantime they are going to continue torturing him, spurs him to take radical action. It's now. Or never.

Perhaps Jason and the rest had no idea of what a man in such extremities might do. Perhaps they thought that Reggie was incapable of any kind of action. It must have been unexpected when Reggie, battered, bloodied and whimpering, leapt to his feet and hurled himself through the closed first-floor window, falling twenty feet. Despite damaging his ankle severely, he managed to stagger to a neighbouring house where he explained his predicament. The police were summoned, but before they arrived the gang made their escape, tumbling out of the house and making off in their flash cars: their BMWs, Mercedes, and Golfs. If the police came for them, they would deny that anything untoward had happened. They would say that Reggie Nunn was making it all up, that there had been some horseplay, and that he had jumped out of the window for a dare.

But the house had been under surveillance for some time as part of Operation Max. Police CCTV cameras had recorded everything that occurred outside 65 Hollands Walk: the arrival of the various gang members, the leap from the window of the terrified Reggie Nunn, his arrival at the neighbouring house in distress with his face cut and bloodied, his ankle shattered. Then there were the shots of the sudden exodus of the gang members dashing for their cars, Jason Vella driving off with a female.

From this day the Vella empire went into decline. There were almost immediate arrests and remands in custody on charges ranging from drug-dealing to serious assault. Even Jason Vella, the untouchable, was charged and for the first time there was a powerful witness to his activities. Other witnesses were sought but of 26 whom the police hoped to get into the witness box only four, encouraged in particular by Detective Constable Paul Keable, agreed to testify, provided that they were given new identities. The others could not bring themselves to risk appearing against the hitherto unassailable Vella. Perhaps their fear was understandable. They knew what happened to anyone who crossed him. There was the man who was shot in the chest at point-blank range with a handgun and who ended up on a life-support machine but even he had not dared to complain to the police. There was the 21-year-old who went to hospital, the backs of his hands burned with a hot iron. Yet he had not reported this to the police. Another was given a 'Glasgow smile' – both sides of his face sliced from the ear to mouth with a Stanley knife – but he too did not go to the police. Then there was the victim of a competition between two of Vella's followers to see who could punch him in the face the hardest. Here was another one too afraid to report what had happened to him.

In the run up to the trials of the principals, the pressure on witnesses and police officers never ceased. There were regular threatening phone calls and menacing letters. Vella still had people on the outside working for him, hoping to torpedo the case. In the face of this, it was an achievement to keep the four witnesses up to the mark and to get them to testify.

At the trial at the maximum security Woolwich Crown Court in June 1995, the court heard a series of accounts of the most alarmingly gratuitous brutality. There was Mark Skeets, a gang member, who went to the Lakeside shopping complex at Thurrock with Jason and two other friends. It was a pleasant enough outing. Then Skeets was invited over for a drink at a place in Corringham, near East Tilbury, where he found a reception committee, a dozen or so gang members all waiting for Skeets, their old chum. He was seized and handcuffed and the front of his head and his eyebrows were shaved. They took off his shoes and socks and stubbed out cigarette butts on the soles of his feet. Then he was jabbed with knives. After this he was forced to snort lines of cocaine and to lick a sheet of 500 LSD tablets. His trousers were removed and he was given a bone and made to kneel and lick a dog's bowl. The contents of a pepper pot were poured down his throat. And all of this was recorded on the Polaroid camera that Skeets had bought earlier in the day with his friend Jason and two others at Lakeside. Finally, he was left on a freezing January evening at One Tree Hill Country Park, completely stoned, barefoot, humiliated and afraid. And why? Because he had had the nerve to send a Christmas card to Jason's girlfriend.

There were other similar tales heard by the jury. One man had his front door kicked in and, despite the fact that there were people in the sitting room, the TV was blasted with a sawn-off shotgun and a CS gas canister was released. But no one reported that incident to the police either. Nor was there any complaint from the man who, after being raped, was taken to a duck pond and made to swim to the middle to catch a duck. Clubs, batons, razors, and baseball bats were weapons of choice on so many of these occasions.

Dean Power was twice punished. Towards the end of 1992, he was whipped with a metal coat hanger and beaten with a bamboo stick. On a second occasion, in October 1993, Vella and a companion went to his home. Here they jabbed him with a toasting fork, beat him with lumps of wood, kicked him in the head, and stamped on his feet and arms. He was totally disfigured.

Power said in court, 'He's like Jekyll and Hyde. The bloke was a lunatic. Seemed a nice bloke at first but he's just possessed, like he had the devil in him or something. Basically now I'm living my whole life in fear.'

The psychopathic Jason Vella was convicted on charges of supplying ecstasy, amphetamine sulphate and cannabis; causing grievous bodily harm with intent to Reg Nunn and Dean Power, and aggravated bodily harm to Alan Bailey and Dean Power, as well as false imprisonment of Dean Power, twice, and Mark Skeets, once. In July 1995 he was sentenced to a total of 17 years for a variety of offences including conspiracy to supply drugs and false imprisonment. Judge Alan Simpson told him: 'You set yourself up as a criminal Czar of south-east Essex. You imposed your will on those who argued with you with a regime of torture and terror. There is no doubt in my mind that many people have breathed more easily since your arrest.' He added that had Vella been only a year or so older he would have received 30 years.

After this, an order was made under the Contempt of Court Act which prevented publication of the convictions and sentences because of other related trials yet to be held. These concerned other members of the gang. News of Vella's sentence was finally released in January 1996 when the last of the Operation Max trials was concluded at Snaresbrook Crown Court. Operation Max ended with 21 prosecutions and Essex police's first witness protection programme.

Vella's closest associate, 22-year-old Simon Renoldi of Chigwell, was given six years eight months after conspiring to supply ecstasy, amphetamine sulphate and cannabis resin. He was also convicted of falsely imprisoning Dean Power. Scott Hunt, 22, of Benfleet was sentenced to five years for conspiring to supply ecstasy. He received a consecutive nine months' sentence for possessing a revolver and four bullets found hidden under a bush in his back garden. James Skeets, 21, of Benfleet, was given two years' imprisonment for conspiring to supply cannabis resin. Anthony Barker, 31, of Wickford, was sentenced to three years for conspiring to supply amphetamine sulphate, and Anthony Dann, 25, of Stanford-le-Hope was given three years for causing grievous bodily harm with intent to Reg Nunn.

These sentences, and in particular that handed out to Vella, were a powerful statement from the authorities that drug dealing on the grand scale must be beaten. Seventeen years for so young a man ought to be a serious deterrent. But though Vella, one of the most unpleasant drugs barons, is locked away, the trade in Essex is as strong as ever. The triple murder of drug dealers Tony Tucker, Patrick Tate and Craig Rolfe in their Range Rover at Rettendon, only a few weeks before these sentences were announced, did nothing to deter the drugs gangsters. The murders served only to emphasize the ruthlessness of those involved. Bear in mind also that none of the proceeds from their activities has been recovered from Vella or his followers. Since then new figures have come on the scene, jostling for supremacy. Some have lasted but a short time, removed by police action or by the savage presence of their competitors. Even as they have disappeared, however, others have stepped into the vacuum and have in turn either prospered or failed.

After completing their sentences, two of Vella's lieutenants, Anthony Dann and Anthony Barker, were almost immediately in trouble with the law. Out in the free world, Barker resumed drug dealing and earned another five years. Dann, who shot a man in a London pub, is now serving a life sentence. But if the authorities are determined to wipe out drug traffickers, the traffickers are equally determined to continue their trade. The drugs campaign set up by the Betts family has not seriously dented the trade. At Basildon and throughout Essex – and throughout the country – clubbers are still taking Ecstasy and amphetamines and are still filling the pockets of the country's most treacherous criminals, the worthless men who sell wretchedness in packets.

The Most Murderous Supergrass

———————— ❖ ————————

Be careful with this man. You'll read his story but you may not wish to believe it. His name is John Henry 'Bruce' Childs. And he's dangerous. Only a few months before this account opens, he was given six life sentences for six murders. Now he is in the witness box as four men whom he has named as accomplices also face charges of murder. But none of the newly accused had ever suspected, so they were to say, that Childs was a violent man and never had they suspected that he would turn supergrass and involve them in the murders.

When he opened the case, in October 1980, David Tudor Price QC, the prosecuting counsel, issued a stark warning to the jury: 'The details of this case are extremely unpleasant,' he said. 'It will be necessary for you to steel yourselves to listen to descriptions which are really revolting.' They were to hear Childs' confession to his part in six murders and his implication of others whom he described as accomplices. The jury was to hear about not just the killings but also the methods by which Childs claimed the bodies of the victims were disposed of. They were to be shown the murder weapons – a Sten gun, a Webley .45, a sword stick, a diver's knife and two firemen's axes – as well the saws and mallets used when disposing of the corpses. Six people who went missing between 1974 and 1978 had never been found. Now Childs was able to tell the world what had happened to them. These were not just 'thrill kills'. The first of them was a matter of business rivalry, but the other five, so Childs would say, were contract killings.

In the dock Childs went back over the history of these dark matters. He had been released from prison in the mid-1970s after serving a sentence for stealing motor bikes. He had gone to work as a van driver for another ex-convict, a Hornchurch man, Terence Pinfold, who had set up a legitimate business making good quality life jackets and underwater diving equipment. As a bank robbery get-away driver, Childs must have been thought quite suitable for his new work. The business was established in the former St Thomas' church hall in Haydon Road in Dagenham. Pinfold's partner was another former convict, 6 ft 6 ins tall Henry MacKenney, and there is every reason to believe that at the time Childs joined them as a delivery man, both men were trying to go straight. Also sharing the premises was Terry 'Teddy Bear' Eve, who made soft toys.

Childs' matter-of-fact account of the first murder is chilling. He described how he, MacKenney, and Pinfold had a conversation about Eve, about how Pinfold wished to take over Eve's business. It was then that they arrived at a solution. It was agreed that Eve should be killed by Childs and MacKenney. Pinfold said that he would reward them with £100 a week.

One evening in November 1974, Terry Eve returned to the workshop. He had been delivering toys to Bob Patience's Barn Restaurant at Braintree. MacKenney and Childs were there, as were Pinfold and Robert Winston Brown, who did odd jobs at the workshop. In his time, Brown had been a modestly successful professional wrestler, appearing as the masked 'White Angel'. No sooner had Eve arrived than he was attacked, beaten senseless with a metal pipe and a length of rubber high-pressure hose. Childs's statement spares little detail. 'I smashed Eve twice in the face with a hammer,' he says. 'He was thrown on the floor and MacKenney jumped on his chest and started hitting Eve in the face with the hammer.' Then MacKenney strangled the victim with a rope. Neither Pinfold nor Brown took part in this murder.

Their intention was then to dismember the body on the premises. Pinfold had purchased an industrial mincing machine for £25 through *Exchange and Mart*. This was of limited use because there was inadequate electric power for it to be effective. The murderers left the workshop with the body while the others cleaned up the floor with five gallons of sulphuric acid provided by Pinfold. MacKenney and Childs took the body to Childs' east

London flat and burnt it in the living room fireplace over a period of 13 hours. Any remaining bones were hammered to powder. Later, as they drove along the Barking by-pass, the murderers scattered the ashes from a small plastic bag through the car window. It had been, according to Childs, 'a difficult murder'.

(At this point it may be fair to stress to the reader that this was the account that 'Bruce' Childs gave to the police and the jury. The men he described as his accomplices always denied the truth of what Childs said.)

To resume: Eve was reported missing and Pinfold and the others were questioned about his disappearance but the police made no progress with their enquiries. Childs now told how murder became a more serious matter. He said that after the Eve murder there was a policy meeting. Really, despite his statement that it had been difficult, Childs was also to imply that in many ways killing in a private warehouse and disposing of a body was not all that much of a problem. There could be money in it. Why not set up in business as contract killers? There was always somebody wanting to get rid of a business rival or a wife or a cast-off lover.

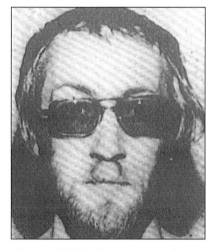
'Bruce' Childs, the most murderous supergrass.

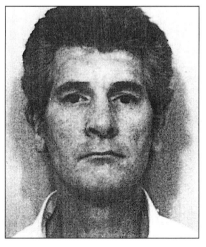
Henry MacKenney, whose sentence for murder was quashed in 2003.

Pinfold, it was decided, would act as the agent. He would tout for business and MacKenney and Childs would do the killing. All disposals would be done in Childs' flat. But what if one of them got cold feet, threatened to squeal? Simple: in that case, if one of them did crack up, then it would be up to the other two to get rid of him. MacKenney was all for the proposal. He was tired of working 'on the pavement' as an armed robber because he was so tall and therefore readily identifiable. Murder was a much better option. It was safer than hold-ups.

But just pause a moment. Does it really seem likely? Are there such wicked people? Well, yes, sadly there are. But was Childs telling the truth?

In court he described the first of the contracts. Leonard Thompson from Upminster had a grudge against George Brett, a haulier and low-level criminal. The two had had a fight and Brett had fractured Thompson's skull with an iron bar. He wanted something done. This, according to Childs, was the first contract. There was some haggling over the fee. Asked for £2,000, Thompson demurred. After he agreed to supply a Sten gun and 200 rounds of ammunition, he was given a 10% discount in a proper business-like arrangement.

In the last week of 1974, a smartly dressed man calling himself Jennings arrived at the farm near Southend where Brett lived. His wife came to the door. The visitor told her that he had some haulage work for her husband. Would she make sure he was home on the following Saturday? On the Saturday, Jennings – this was Childs in a city gent's costume – called again at the farm. The job was in Dagenham, he told Brett. Would he come and have a look at what had to be done? Brett asked him to lead the way. He'd follow in his own car. Just as Brett was starting his Mercedes, Terry, his 10 year old son, ran out and climbed in with his father. They followed Childs to the workshop in Haydon Road. Neither father nor son was seen again although some days later the car was found near King's Cross station.

In court, Childs described what occurred in the workshop. It took only three of the 200 Sten gun rounds to complete the job. First, MacKenney shot George Brett who fell to the floor. For some reason – a warped compassion? – Childs gave the boy a worn teddy bear to hold. 'He just stood rigid looking. I grabbed hold of him to stop him going to his father and finding him dead. Then MacKenney shot his father again, went over to me, and shot the little boy in the head as I held him in my arms.' Then off they took the bodies to Childs' flat.

Despite rumours about what had happened to Brett and his son, no one was arrested. The police were bemused. Where were the Bretts? Had George Brett been a police informer? Had he stumbled on a crime syndicate ready to take over the remainder of the Kray's operations? Was he the victim of the notorious Tibbs gang? There was even the suggestion that Brett had been inquiring too deeply into the Mountnessing bullion robbery, in which his brother John and three others, including George Ince had been involved.

The next killing, in November 1975, was not a contract job. It was a matter of security. The victim, Robert Brown, the 'White Angel', had escaped from Chelmsford prison, where he was serving a short sentence. He had been allowed to hide out in the workshop, sleeping there on a camp bed. Then Childs told how he and the two others began to worry about what might happen if he was recaptured. Might he tell what he knew about the murder of

George Brett.

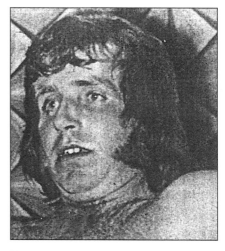

Terence Eve.

Eve? Brown was lured to Childs' council flat, where he and MacKenney killed him. He was shot twice in the back of the head but not immediately killed. There was a struggle. Then he was stabbed with a knife and a sword. After this he was hit with an axe but went on fighting against the two men he had believed to be his friends. At last, they got him, running him through with a sword-stick. As he lay on the floor, still struggling, he was finally impaled, the blade of the sword-stick passing through the polythene sheets which Childs had put down to catch the blood, and into the floorboards. And no one heard? Remarkable.

Brown's ashes were scattered on Wanstead Flats. Then there was a hiatus. The murders and disappearances suddenly stopped. Childs was away on a two-year stretch for burglary. Why, one wonders, did MacKenney not just get on with the contracts himself?

In July 1978, Paul Morton-Thurtle consulted Childs, out on the street again. He had fallen out with a business colleague. Frederick Sherwood ran a nursing home in Herne Bay. He owed money to Morton-Thurtle and was refusing to pay it back. Could anything be done? Of course, Childs told him. Anything could be done for a price. Morton-Thurtle agreed the price of £4,000, paid in instalments of £1,500 down and £500 a fortnight. When Sherwood advertised his car for sale he was invited by a prospective purchaser to visit him. When he turned up at MacKenney's bungalow, near the workshop, he was given £480 for the car. After the transaction, as he sat drinking tea and counting the money, Childs hit him with a 2 lb hammer and MacKenney shot him. The car was later found at Earls Court, but there was never any sign of Sherwood.

On 12th October 1978, the last of the murders was committed. Ronnie Andrews, a roof repairer, disappeared. Police enquiries revealed that he had been having troubles with his wife. She had a boyfriend. When police spoke to his close friend – Henry MacKenney – he confirmed that Andrews had personal and business problems. He suggested that perhaps Ronnie Andrews had just moved out of the district. But Childs put a further gloss on the story. It was MacKenney who was having an affair with Gwen Andrews. Her husband had never suspected MacKenney, who had persuaded him to meet a private detective and employ him to discover evidence about his wife's affair. He agreed to do so and went to Childs' flat. Here MacKenney shot Andrews through the head with a revolver fitted with a silencer. Afterwards, as he handed over £400 to Childs for his help, MacKenney confided to his accomplice that he was sorry he had to kill his friend.

The following day Ronnie Andrews' Lincoln Continental was found in the River Nene in Lincolnshire. There was a half-empty bottle of vodka on the back seat. Had Andrews accidentally driven into the river while drunk? Had his body been swept out to sea by the strong tides? That was the general police conclusion.

In his evidence to the court in October 1980, Childs became the first serial killer in modern times to confess to such awful crimes and give evidence against his alleged accomplices. Why did he do so? Was it because he had been apprehended yet again, this time in a security van raid? Was it that as an incorrigible criminal he feared a sentence of up to 20 years? Why, the police asked, would Childs make it all up? He had nothing to gain. There would be no early release for him. After confessing to what he had done, he could expect nothing less than life, a life sentence from which there could be no release. Was it because he was deeply distressed with guilt? Did the murder of 10-year-old Terry Brett haunt him, as he said it did? Did he feel such things deeply?

Let's have a look at this man, this 41 year old in the dock, his metal framed spectacles reflecting the light, the short beard partially concealing the mouth. And remember that MacKenney and Pinfold, Thompson and Morton-Thurtle all claimed to be totally unaware of who had done these killings.

Let's hear Childs talking about himself and his neighbours. In the courtroom Childs did not hesitate to say how he dealt with neighbours who bothered him. He had put an axe through one door; he had thrown bricks through windows; he had slashed car tyres when he had been blocked in. The Alsatian dog of one neighbour had annoyed him and he had shot it with a crossbow. 'It had no particular importance to me,' Childs commented. 'It was rather an insignificant act compared to some of the things I have done.'

And look in his flat. Look on the walls. There are more than 20 weapons there, used as decoration. There are bayonets, axes, a spear-gun, a French cavalry sword, knives, daggers, a club, and a sword-stick which was used in one of the murders. He confessed that some of the weapons had been used to kill the victims and had been put back up on the wall after being soaked and cleaned in bleach.

Here he is in court replying to a question as to how he feels about what had happened in his flat. He has no feelings about it, and he is impatient with a question about the precise timing of the murders. 'I would like to point out,' he says, 'that you don't keep looking at a stop-watch when you are murdering someone'.

Remember that months earlier, in December 1979, Childs had pleaded guilty to six murders and was given six life sentences. Now, in the following year, he was appearing at the Old Bailey as prosecution witness against the four men he had implicated. Michael Mansfield QC, defending MacKenney, impressed upon the jury that the case against his client rested almost entirely upon the word of Childs, a man he described as 'maniacally obsessed in thoughts and actions by violence'. A psychologist, Barry Irving, commenting on whether it was safe to rely on Childs' evidence, said, 'He fits, on his own admission and on his performance in court, nine-tenths of the classic description of a psychopath'. One of the characteristics of psychopaths is that they are able to sustain complicated fabrications over a long period. Childs almost certainly had the capacity to fabricate evidence. So there were strong reasons to doubt Childs' accounts of the murders, especially in the absence of any witnesses, forensic evidence, or bodies.

It's a hideous case and, after a trial lasting 37 days, the verdicts brought in were as controversial as the narratives had been shocking. Was Childs telling the truth? He said that all four men were involved in murders. If he was telling the truth, all four defendants were guilty on all charges. In his summing-up, Mr Justice May warned the jury that Childs could not be regarded as a reliable witness because of contradictions in some of his accounts. To convict on the evidence of a self-confessed killer alone would be unwise and dangerous, the judge said, alerting them to the need to consider corroborative evidence. But was there enough corroborative evidence? In the end the jury arrived at confused conclusions.

For instance, in the Eve case, Pinfold was said to have planned the murder, although he took no part in it. Nevertheless, Pinfold was found guilty of murder. His alibi that he was in Clacton with his wife and family on the weekend of Eve's murder was dismissed by the judge. In Childs' lurid account, MacKenney had strangled the victim but he was found not guilty because there was no corroborating evidence. Leonard Thomson, who, according to Childs, had paid for the murder of Brett, was found not guilty, but, on Childs' word alone, the jury convicted MacKenney although there was no corroborating evidence in this instance either.

Childs had given evidence that the wrestler Robert Brown, who was said to have witnessed the Eve murder, was murdered by Pinfold and MacKenney but the jury brought in 'Not guilty' verdicts. How is it that Childs' statements were accepted in some instances and not in others? As for the murder of Sherwood, the verdict was equally illogical. The jury decided that Paul Morton-Thurtle, who allegedly had asked MacKenney to kill Sherwood, was innocent. But MacKenney was found guilty.

MacKenney and Pinfold were both given life sentences. There was a recommendation in MacKenney's case that he serve not less than 25 years.

In the years after the trial, there were doubts about the jury's conclusions and both men continued protesting their innocence. In 1981 and in 1987 their appeals were lost and they were denied leave to appeal again. In Pinfold's case, had he admitted his guilt, it is likely that he would have been released as early as 1993. From time to time, Childs wrote affidavits completely absolving Pinfold from involvement in any of the murders. He confessed to other prisoners that MacKenney, whom he hated, was also innocent. At other times he retracted his admissions.

In the late 1990s, the Criminal Cases Review Commission took up the case and a renewed appeal went before the Court of Criminal Appeal in October 2003, when both MacKenney and Pinfold were freed on bail by the Court of Criminal Appeal. What the appeal judges considered were factors such as Childs' mental state which was concealed from the jury when the case was heard.

In December 2003, the sentences of MacKenney and Pinfold, both now in their seventies, were finally quashed. The appeal judges said that the evidence against them was 'so unreliable that it is worthless'.

One major mystery remains: was Terry Eve really murdered? Bert Wickstead, the Head of Serious Crimes at Scotland Yard, is alleged to have been told by fellow officers that Eve was alive and living in south London under an assumed name and that he, Wickstead, rejected the suggestion on the grounds that, if it were true, the reputation of the CID would be damaged. There were suggestions that Eve had been about to be charged with a £75,000 stereo heist and that if found guilty he would have served five years. So, some said he had simply disappeared. It does not seem likely but, even so, had the jury been apprised of the possible doubt in this case, Pinfold would have walked free, and possibly the whole of Childs' testimony against the others would have collapsed. And so perhaps would the supergrass system which had been pronounced such a success in this case. It is ironic, of course, that these matters were all known to the court at the time of the trial.

Neither MacKenney nor Pinfold is an angel. Earlier they had both served prison sentences. They were genuine Essex villains, but neither deserved to spend more than 20 years of life rotting away behind bars.

But who was responsible for the other disappearances? Childs alone? Or Childs and another? If some of the murders did not take place in the Haydon Road workshop, where were they committed? Did Childs alone – or with another – really have such a struggle with Brown in his flat? Did no one hear them? And what about the burning of the bodies in the flat? Did no one ever smell anything? Childs' accounts creak. They creak now and they must have creaked a quarter of a century ago. And there's still the mystery of what really happened to the missing five men and the ten-year-old boy. It's a dreadful case and odd in more than one particular.

HONOUR AMONG THIEVES

———————❀———————

They make an interesting group. First, there's Michael Gervaise, six feet tall, and wonderfully described as 'a balding figure with the mild air of a retail tobacconist'. You can just imagine him, can't you? You wouldn't think that he was a fluent linguist, a high liver, who tripped back and forth to Europe's finest hotels and best restaurants. One of his chums has said, with an undisguised tone of admiration, 'Micky used to fly to Paris and back just for afternoon tea.' Furthermore he is highly skilled when it comes to burglar alarms. That is, he is an expert at putting them out of action. He has used his skill particularly successfully in jewellers and bank vaults, and is one of the country's leading burglars. On his payroll he has two burglar alarm specialists who work for legitimate firms and pass on useful information. For the most part, despite his activity, Gervaise has kept out of police hands. His record is unblemished, save for 18 months' imprisonment for taking part in the 1975 Bank of America robbery.

Then, there are Lennie Gibson and the two Agudas, Rudolpho and Renalto, all three of them Freemasons. Lennie, who has a property empire of rented apartments, had risen high in Masonic ranks and is master of Waterways Lodge. He certainly enjoys a fine life; not many people in the 1970s have a detached house with a swimming pool. Oh yes, and he is one of London's most violent criminals. In fact, in a secret police file entitled 'The top 100 most dangerous armed robbers in London', Lennie Gibson is number 42. And Rudolpho 'Dolph' Aguda is a close associate, an experienced robber with an equally respectable front as a successful businessman. His nephew, Renaldo 'Ron' Aguda, specialises in uncoupling trailers from their tractor units at speed, a skill which has often been found useful.

Micky Sewell, an old friend of Gervaise, makes up the team. He is another well-known underworld figure. He has recently been released on bail of £200,000 while on a charge of armed robbery. That enormous surety indicates that – like the others – where Sewell is, there is money.

That's the team, then, the five of them. At least, they are the main players. There are also the mysterious Nick and Roger, never identified, who will turn up on the day and play their part. And let's not forget some others behind the scenes, such as the corrupt policemen who over the years have proved such a support to various members of the criminal fraternity or the office manager at the haulage company who has passed on information about transport timings.

On 24th March 1980, this gang managed to steal 321 ingots of silver bullion valued at £3.4 million from a container on its way from the vaults in Tooley Street, just south of the river, to Tilbury Docks. They have had less publicity than the Great Train Robbers but their achievement – is that the right word? – was more significant. They carried out what was then Britain's biggest armed robbery. In daylight.

It had taken some planning, of course. The information had to be right, for a start. No good turning up for a job and finding the cupboard was bare. They needed copper-bottomed information from inside. After all, they were after a big prize. So, the container left Tooley Street when and at what time? And what about security? What kind of transport would be used? Crikey, an ordinary container van? Not an armoured van? And how many guards would there be? Two? Only two? Travelling behind in a saloon car? And they'd be unarmed? Unbelievable! What about the police? Would they be about? No, nobody bothered to let the police know about these runs. Perhaps they never felt it was necessary. It was a piece of cake, or looked like it, anyway. What on earth would the East German government have made of it? It was their silver after all.

To play his part Michael Gervaise had to find himself a police uniform, and there was a crooked sergeant in the Met who was able to help out. Then there were the white, official-looking coats for Ron Aguda and Micky Sewell. With all the preparations, it must have cost them a few bob but they were well within budget. Four of the gang – not young Ron – had contributed £1,000 each towards running costs.

It all started off mid-morning at Tooley Street, with what the driver with his 10,000 kilo load of silver must have believed was just another routine run to the docks. It is likely that the guards never noticed the white Ford van which overtook them as they set off. Even if they had, they would not have recognized Lennie Gibson or his passenger Dolph Aguda. It was a few minutes after eleven o'clock when Gibson and Dolph drove into the Ripple Road lay-by on the A13 at Barkingside. The haul was on the way, they told the others.

Then a policeman and a man from the Ministry of Transport – or somebody official like that, because he was wearing a long white coat – began putting out the traffic cones. Passing drivers would congratulate themselves that they had just escaped being pulled over for some ridiculous traffic census, while Dolph Aguda and Michael Gervaise, both sporting false moustaches, arranged the cones and wondered just how long the container would take. What if another police car saw them and pulled in for a chat? Then Ron – that's young Aguda – arrived in a red Transit van, accompanied by Nick and Roger. They were all there now. But where was the container? Come on.

And then it comes into view. And Michael Gervaise steps out into the road, holding up his hand, flagging down the container, waving it through the traffic cones and into the lay-by. The security men in their saloon follow him. Gervaise strolls over to the container, and so do the two men in white coats. Ron Aguda, looking the part with his clipboard, asks the driver to switch off his engine. It's a Ministry traffic check, he says. Can he have a word? The driver climbs down from his cab and the security guards, wondering, clamber out of the saloon. Lennie Gibson and the other two go across to them. The sawn-off shotgun comes out. Any messing about, any attempt to be a hero, and they'll be knee-capped. Understand? And does the driver understand? He does. There is no resistance.

The three prisoners, guarded by Sewell and Roger, were put in the back of the Transit. Gervaise drove them off, first to

Lennie Gibson, senior Freemason and one of London's most violent criminals.

Greenwich Park. They waited an hour or so, to give Ron time to drive the container to his Walthamstow haulage yard. The driver and the guards were then taken to a lock-up garage in Deptford, from where they were released some time later. Dolph Aguda and Gibson disposed of the white Ford.

Some weeks later, the silver was transferred to a 'slaughter' – a hiding place for stolen goods – a rented lock-up garage near Oakwood station at the northern end of the Piccadilly line. Only Dolph Aguda and Lennie Gibson knew where it was hidden and they each kept a key. The gang had agreed not to touch the silver for two months after which Lennie Gibson would make arrangements for its sale and that is where it was to have ended. Job done, no point hanging around. They were all busy people. They all had other work to do, other robberies to get on with.

It is a village, the underworld. Everybody knows bits about everybody else's business. But for most of the time they rub along, get on with their own lives. There are rumours, of course, rivalries, too. And there are loyalties, but how often these prove to be frail. After all, if it comes to the crunch and the police have you stone cold and they're promising you a long stay in prison unless … Unless what? Unless you can be helpful to them. That may be the wisest thing to do. Be helpful. Even if it means giving up your pals. There's money, too, on offer for those who can really deliver. And a reward of £300,000 put up by insurers after the silver bullion robbery was very tempting.

Now, in the village that is the underworld, one thing often quite unintentionally leads to another. After a bank robbery at East Finchley in which a guard was shot, the police successfully rounded up those responsible, and a chain reaction began. One of the gang, promised a severe sentence, offered up details not only of the East Finchley robbery but also of other villains and other jobs. The trail led to Tony Fiori, a burglar of considerable talents. When he was brought in to answer questions, he too, anxious to save himself from a long term inside, volunteered information. He knew something about the silver bullion raid, he said. After all, Michael Gervaise was an old friend.

It was convenient for the police that at the time Michael Gervaise was in custody, being questioned about a number of major burglaries. Now he was asked about the silver bullion. For four days he refused to make any comment. Then he was put in a cell with Fiori. Gervaise knew Fiori had told the police what he knew about the silver bullion. He offered his old pal £25,000 if he would retract his story. But Fiori, that loyal old friend, told the police all that had transpired.

Under questioning, Gervaise now admitted to some of the crimes he was being asked about. However, he would say nothing about the silver or about a recent raid at Hatton Garden. Even if they sent him to prison, if he remained silent he would have his share when he came out.

But finally Gervaise decided to turn supergrass. If he could bargain with the details of some of his offences, if he gave other useful information too, then he would be given a relatively light sentence. He'd be able to enjoy himself after only a few years' imprisonment. Gervaise's confessions led to the arrest of many of his old colleagues but it didn't quite turn out as he intended. The police were after information on the silver bullion robbery. Nothing else would do. It was a case of silver bullion or no deal, and finally Gervaise admitted to being in on the silver bullion

The 'slaughter' at Oakwood where police found the silver bullion.

robbery. But he didn't know where the silver was hidden, he told his interrogators. Well, who did? Who was with him? They were pressing him hard now, making him understand that there might be a deal, a shorter sentence if he could be more specific. Lennie Gibson and Dolph Aguda were now arrested, each with the keys of the Oakwood 'slaughter' in their pockets, but the likelihood is that the most helpful information about their involvement came not from Michael Gervaise but from another source. Micky Sewell steps back into the limelight now and so does Roy Garner.

As soon as he had heard about the arrest from a friendly police officer, Micky Sewell had feared that Gervaise might implicate him. Perhaps he ought to leave the country. If they arrested him, he'd be in very serious trouble because he was out on bail. He had therefore sought out another old pal, Roy Garner. He would help. Roy knew how to get round difficulties. He understood things. Roy even knew about the silver bullion job. In fact, he'd been invited to take part, and no offence had been taken when he had turned down the offer. So Micky Sewell went to enlist the aid of his old chum.

Roy Garner was a very significant criminal, always into serious crime. He was a hold-up man but was also involved in gold fraud and cocaine dealing on a grand scale. He was very wealthy, the owner of a nightclub and a stud. His home was palatial and he lived in high style. But of course, high style has to be paid for, and it was paid for in part by his criminal activities and in part by the significant sums he received for information which he gave to police, banks, and insurance companies. Over the years he had been rewarded for his information about various jobs, six in the past five years – among them a Brinks Mat security van hold-up in Hampstead and a massive fraudulent insurance claim based on a faked robbery. Garner is said to have amassed over £500,000 from this kind of information. His handler, Detective Superintendent Tony Lundy, recommended him for these rewards on the strength of what he told the police. Now, there was a £300,000 reward for information about the silver bullion robbery. Roy Garner was determined to have a share of it. That Micky Sewell trusted him mattered not. A friendship which had survived the years counted for nothing. Garner informed Lundy what Sewell had told him about the robbery and those involved. Those now under arrest knew the game was up and that they might as well cooperate with their interrogators.

On 3rd June, ten weeks after the robbery, Lennie Gibson led the police to the lock-up garage at Oakwood where the silver, all 10 tons of it, was stacked. That there were a dozen ingots worth £120,000 missing remains a mystery. But Roy Garner, the informant recorded in official police records as 'Dave Grainger', received his reward money, as ever on the recommendation of Tony Lundy.

There has been much said and written about Lundy and his close links with Garner and other criminals. Lundy's robbery squad solved hundreds of robberies, and many criminals were imprisoned as a result of his energies. He persuaded many robbers not only to confess but also to 'grass' on their accomplices. But was he 'bent or brilliant'? Certainly, the reputation of Scotland Yard and of Lundy suffered when certain facts came out at the silver bullion trial. If the most active team of armed hold-up men was shattered, so too was the Yard with another series of corruption investigations.

In court, for instance, Gervaise told how Freemasons in the police warned his accomplices of their imminent arrest. Of eight members in Gibson's Lodge, six retired early from the police service. It is fair to say that Gibson – just like that other Worshipful Master Kenneth Noye in another lodge – was expelled from the Freemasons.

One version of the trial has it that Lundy advised the gang members how to plead in court. He suggested that they might, if they were cooperative, be sentenced to seven years. Dolph Aguda was recommended to express his shame and sorrow at taking part in the robbery. He had put his past behind him he was told to say. Now he was a hard-working man, a successful businessman, who had contributed much to charities. The impression he was to give was that it was a lapse. Gibson, for his part, was advised to tell the court that he had been foolish, that he had been tempted. He was to swear that he would never be involved in any criminal activities in the future. He admitted to having a criminal record but said that for the past ten years he was a reformed man. The court was not told by the investigating officers about his being number 42 in the list of most dangerous armed robbers.

The men's lawyers took similar lines. Their clients were 'amateurs of crime', they claimed, all of them quite out of their depth in such complex criminal activities.

Mr Justice Miskin seems to have taken heed of what the accused and their lawyers said. In the case of Gibson and the Agudas, he intended, so he said, to reduce their sentences significantly. They must have been disappointed, however, when he announced sentences of ten years each. Whilst this was lighter than the normal tariff for such an offence, they had been led to expect an even lighter term of imprisonment. Michael Gervaise for his cooperation received a sentence of five years.

The mystery of the missing ingots remains. At first the silver was hidden in Ron Aguda's haulage yard in Walthamstow. It was only after Gervaise was arrested that it was moved, shuttled, a dozen bars at a time, to the Oakwood 'slaughter'. Did one of the robbers take them as his share? Could they have been taken by a corrupt policeman during the raid? This seems unlikely: they were too heavy to move without being noticed. Was anyone paid off before the raid, told to help himself? Now that is an interesting possibility. It remains a fascinating mystery.

In 1984 Roy Garner, now unprotected by the police who had looked after him for so much of his career, was sentenced to 22 years, reduced to 16 years on appeal, on drug trafficking charges. Micky Sewell's indiscretions to Garner had led to the unravelling of the plot. But he was not arrested for many months. He was never charged with taking part in the silver robbery, as the principal witness against him, Michael Gervaise, was now wholly discredited. Instead he came before court on another charge and was given three years.

And that wrapped it up as far as the gang was concerned. It was Scotland Yard which now, in the light of revelations about police corruption, had to investigate its own internal criminality.

ROTHERMEL

———————— ❁ ————————

It was a gangland tip-off that led to the finding of the body. For 17 months since the winter of 1987, there had been no sign of Bernie Burns although there was every expectation that he was dead. Now, out of the blue in July 1988, came the information which took police and dogs to a quiet copse at Long Spring Wood in Little Baddow. The body, wrapped in a rotting red blanket, lay in a shallow grave. There was no head and no hands. Whoever was responsible had tried to make identification difficult but leaving a corpse in a shallow grave is perhaps one of the least effective ways of disposal. Even though the missing parts never turned up, it was a simple matter to check hospital x-rays of Burns' spine with what remained of him.

Why had this 26-year-old small-time London criminal been killed? There were suggestions that he had annoyed The Firm, the title conferred by the tabloid press on a gang whose principal figures, Tony Tucker, Patrick Tate and Craig Rolfe, were among Essex's most infamous racketeers. Bernie Burns was a man who perhaps knew too much and was incapable of keeping quiet about it. The Firm – the term is used for convenience – had little patience with anyone who made a nuisance of himself and they certainly had within their ranks a man who particularly disliked Burns, a man who could be persuaded to do away with him. Pierre St Ange, a 6 ft 4 ins black man, was a formidable figure, who played American football with the London Ravens. He was employed by Tucker and his colleagues as a doorman at one of the clubs they controlled, Hollywood's in Romford. Recently St Ange had gone to live with Burns' ex-wife, Pamela, in Ilford. But Burns, still in love with her, constantly called at the flat. It was too much for St Ange. 'The little runt', as he called him, had to be taught a lesson. What is not certain is the degree to which he was urged on by his gangster employers. It is certain, however, that Burns was savagely beaten up at the flat and then strangled. His body was wrapped in a red blanket and then taken in the boot of a car to Long Spring Wood and placed in a hastily dug grave.

Then, in the summer of 1988, the police were told not only the whereabouts of the body, but they also learnt about St Ange. And whilst the informant was not sure if a third man had been present when Burns was throttled, he was in no doubt that there was a second man. Enter 29 year old Mark Rothermel from Chelmsford. Perhaps while the police continue their search for Burns' killers, we may pause to look at Rothermel's background.

After dropping out of his London University chemistry degree course, Mark Rothermel worked for his wealthy father as a trainee architect. But he had an adventurous streak and first came to prominence in Essex in 1985 when he told the *Essex Chronicle* of his plans to accompany an expedition in the Congo to find a descendant of the dinosaurs, the Mokele-Mbembe, an African version of the Loch Ness monster which was said to inhabit uncharted swamps. Dr Bill Gibbons, the expedition leader, had met Rothermel two years earlier, shortly after the young man had returned from an expedition to the Amazon with his father. Dr Gibbons later described the young man as 'a very personable individual and highly intelligent with extensive knowledge of several branches of science and medicine'. Nevertheless, in spite of his taste for adventure, it seems altogether incongruous that this well-educated, well-spoken man, training to be an architect, should take himself off to the clubs at night to work as a bouncer. He had honed his body to extreme physical fitness at the gym and he could hold his own at the clubland doors with little difficulty. He worked at several clubs, including the notorious Raquel's in Basildon. But what inclined him to this work? What was it that persuaded him now to abandon architecture for a life which involved not a little brutality and a considerable degree of criminality? It is difficult to understand how it was that Mark Rothermel felt no sort of distaste for his bosses, for those whom he was to meet and with whom he was to socialize in this new world of dropped aitches, thick wads of cash and extreme violence.

And now came the friendship with fellow doorman, Pierre St Ange, the disappearance and later discovery of Bernie Burns, and the police search for the two men described in the *Sun*'s usual breathless prose as 'two Rambo-mad members of a ruthless mob called The Firm'.

While St Ange was soon picked up, Rothermel was less easily found. Police warnings announced that he was 'very, very dangerous' and that he 'would not hesitate to use extreme violence to escape capture'. Police forces throughout the country were advised to use armed officers if they should try to arrest him. For a week there was no indication of where Rothermel might be but then the police learnt that he was hiding out in a little visited stretch of woodland at Danbury. It was hardly surprising he should be there for he had known the area well from childhood.

While armed men searched the wood on foot, a helicopter skimmed over the trees and the pilot spotted some movement on the surface of a pond. Over the loud speaker the helicopter pilot called 'Come out, come out.' Down below the police surrounded the pond where Mark Rothermel, huge and muscular, stood up to his neck in the water. Out he came, dripping mud, his hands above his head. He was wearing combat boots and a camouflage jacket. He'd been living in a broken down caravan in the wood, using survival techniques he had developed in the Congo and on the Amazon.

Rothermel and St Ange were tried at the Old Bailey in November 1989. The court heard how after Burns was killed the two men had buried the body at Long Spring Wood, well-known to Rothermel who in his teenage years had gone there with his girlfriends. The jury was told that after his arrest St Ange had told the police that Rothermel had strangled Burns but later, when giving evidence, he retracted this statement, claiming that he had made it under police pressure. In the end the jury accepted that whilst the two men in the dock were present at the murder it was a third unnamed man who had done the killing and both Rothermel and St Ange refused to give his name.

When, after ten hours, the verdict of guilty of manslaughter but not of murder was returned, the judge, Mr Justice Lowry, told St Ange: 'You participated in an attack on Burns, the former husband of your woman. Another man was the more violent. You

Long Spring Wood where the body of Burns was found. (Robert Hallmann)

know that man's identity but have not spoken up during the trial. You were the one who initiated the attack. I deal with you on the basis that you were not the person who calculated the method of disposal of the body.' St Ange was sentenced to ten years' imprisonment.

Addressing himself to Rothermel who was found guilty only of disposing of the body, the judge observed: 'You were physically active in helping with the burial. It could not have been carried out by one man alone. It was conducted in dreadful, gruesome circumstances.' Certainly the circumstances were gruesome. Rothermel admitted to a friend that he had used an axe on the body. 'The hands came off easily,' he said, 'but the head was more of a problem because of the veins in the neck.' A considered comment from a well brought up boy. He was given six years' imprisonment.

Peter Dean from Rainham, who gave evidence for the prosecution, was given three months for assisting an offender, after admitting helping to conceal Burns' clothing. But he was not the mysterious unidentified third man. It is still not known who this might have been. Some have questioned whether there ever was such a person.

At this point Mark Rothermel disappeared behind prison walls until 1992. But then, what? Did he go straight? Perhaps. There is no record of his being involved in anything dubious in the years immediately after his release. And then, six years later, he comes to public notice again in a quite bizarre escapade in the Congo Republic. He has returned to that part of Africa but it does not seem that this time he had gone seeking some mythical beast. Whatever his reason for being there, Rothermel is in a land torn apart in a fierce civil war. It is a nightmare of massacres on a monstrous scale, of frightening dislocation for the civilian population, of murderous looting forays, of arbitrary justice and of universal chaos. Then he finds himself in prison in Brazzaville, and one day, during a gun battle in the town between police and soldiers, he and about 40 others escape in the confusion. News of this comes back to Britain.

The Foreign Office seems unsure of who he is, this Rothermel chap. All they know is that since November 1998 he has been detained by the Congolese without charge. All they can now say is that he is safe and in contact with the British consul in Brazzaville. Can it be the same Mark Rothermel who was sent to prison some years earlier? What is he doing there? The papers muse on the matter. Then the Foreign Office report that he is an 'aid worker' on a project for a charity called Mission Aid. Other unconfirmed reports come out suggesting that Rothermel is being held for spying. Has he been in contact with the rebels during the civil war? Is he a mercenary? Or is he there with an eye to future business? The Congo is a mineral-rich country. There might be good pickings for anyone with a sharp mind and a tough outlook.

So is he a gangster, a spy, a mercenary, a charity worker or an adventurer? Bernard O'Mahoney, who knows him, has said that he wouldn't be a mercenary. 'The only mercenary work he's ever done is working for £45 a night at Raquel's,' O'Mahoney says.

'He told me that he was going to the Congo to go trekking and to do a bit of charity work.' But according to the Charity Commission, Mission Aid ceased to exist in 1997. Perhaps it was no more than his undeniable thirst for the exotic, for adventure, for testing himself physically, that led him to the Congo. Further questioning at the time elicited little more from the Foreign Office. He had reported to the British consul and then vanished. 'We are not in contact with him now and we do not know where he is,' said a spokesman for the Foreign Office.

To return to O'Mahoney again for another attempt to understand Rothermel. He tells us that: 'He's the sort of feller who couldn't hack doing eight hour shifts or any similar regular job. Mark thrives on excitement and the challenge of doing the unthinkable. That's why he has found himself involved in bizarre incidents about the world, not because he is a career criminal or a ruthless thug.'

That just about wraps up this curious interlude in the unusual life of Mark Rothermel and he disappears again from the public eye. But not for long. In May 2001 he is under arrest yet again, and in Britain, along with several others. This time it's a matter of importing drugs into Britain with a street value of £500,000. He has been arrested at eight o'clock in the morning, following an operation by almost 100 armed policemen and customs officers on the beach at Bawdsey, near Woodbridge, in which quantities of cocaine and cannabis are seized. In all, ten defendants, including two women, are charged.

The accused appeared initially at Ipswich Crown Court. There was a strong presence of armed policemen both inside and outside the court, although that did not deter Rothermel from attempting to vault over the dock. Whether he had any hope of escape or whether he was simply making a dramatic gesture has not been satisfactorily answered. Eventually, in January and February 2002, the case was heard at Woolwich Crown Court. The charges related to the organisation and systematic planning of the importation of 3.3 kilograms of amphetamine and 40 kilograms of high-grade herbal cannabis. Rothermel's lawyers had requested that the trial should not take place at Chelmsford in case memories of his links with the Burns' murder should prejudice his position.

The court heard of a highly sophisticated plan, devised by Mark Rothermel, to pick up drugs in Holland and bring them over to some secluded beach on the east coast for unloading. After that, the drugs would be transported elsewhere and made ready for distribution. But first Rothermel had sought a team. A boat designer was needed to design a super-craft, and there had to be someone to pilot it. And other reliable team members were to be recruited. A suitable landing place was to be decided upon. It took several months for the plan to be put into operation.

The team was a colourful bunch, trustworthy and experienced, a mixture of expertise and muscle. Leonard 'Pugwash' Haworth was a specialist, a renowned designer of first-class power boats, who provided Rothermel with his craft and prepared it for its journey to Holland and back. Over the years he had designed boats at his Isle of Wight boatyard for drug traffickers and black-marketeers and he had served more than one prison term for drug smuggling. Angel Jiminez, a Frenchman, had already shared an unsuccessful smuggling venture and a cell in France with Haworth. He was an expert speedboat sailor whom his old cell mate was able to recommend. Sean Clarke, the second in command, was the front-of-house manager at the Venue night club in Ilford. He drove a Ferrari with personalised number plates. His girlfriend was a page 3 girl. Other members of the gang were Bryan Richardson, a Basildon man; Guy Clements from Dagenham; John McCann from Romford; and Matthew Howes from Grays. Howes, a scaffolder, and Clements, a plumber, worked part-time as doormen at the Venue night club.

In the early months of 2001 Rothermel and his team sought the perfect spot where a speedboat, loaded with drugs, could land its cargo away from the gaze of law enforcers. They looked at a number of likely spots along the coast from Kent up to Norfolk. Places were assessed for remoteness, ease of access, and strength of mobile phone reception. In the end it was Bawdsey, a Suffolk hamlet with a pretty quayside and a quiet beach, which scored 10 out of 10. Point Clear, near St Osyth, was chosen for the launch and as the landing spot to which Jiminez would return after unloading the drugs at Bawdsey.

Remote Point Clear, near St Osyth, chosen as one of the rendezvous points.
(Robert Hallmann)

Meanwhile, in Berkshire, Leonard Haworth, helped by Richardson, loaded the 'Interceptor' boat he had selected for the operation onto a trailer and drove it to a remote farm at Wickford for modifications.

On 1st May Rothermel and Bryan Richardson went to Holland via Dover and Zebrugge. The same day Angel Jimenez set off in the speedboat from Point Clear and arrived at Breskens where he met Rothermel and Richardson. They loaded the drugs, storing them in seven secret compartments in the hull. Once this task was completed, Rothermel and Richardson returned home, this time via the Channel Tunnel, while Jimenez took off on the second leg of his 18-hour round-trip, aiming to arrive at the Suffolk coast early on the morning of 3rd May. Sitting in a pick-up truck in the shingle car-park behind the sea wall at Bawdsey were Clements, Howes, Clarke, and Rothermel awaiting Angel's arrival. They were unaware that Jimenez, the expert sailor, was already in the Deben, quite near them, but had run out of fuel.

And they waited and waited ... until the arrival at Bawdsey of the 100-strong force of customs officers and policemen from the Essex, Norfolk, Suffolk, and Kent forces.

The four men, surrounded, were ordered to lie on the ground. Only Clarke, claiming to be a fisherman, refused at first. He shortly complied after being sprayed with CS gas. Local resident Lilian Lloyd said that the arrival of police and customs men was like something from a movie. She had never seen anything like it in Bawdsey. 'We have had Borstal boys around here when they have escaped, but nothing of this sort of magnitude,' she said. 'It was all a bit unnerving, but once we knew what was happening, it was a different matter. We felt glad that it was so well organized by the police.'

Whilst the men were under arrest at Bawdsey, a customs boat arrived to pick up Angel Jimenez who was floundering just off shore. Meanwhile, down at Point Clear, John McCann, his walkie-talkie at the ready, was expecting Jimenez to arrive as soon as he had offloaded the drugs. And he went on waiting, until he too was arrested by police. He had in his possession a piece of paper with contact numbers of all of the other members of the gang.

At the house belonging to Rothermel's lady friend, there was a considerable amount of property belonging to the mastermind, including a global positioning system (for boat navigation via satellite) as well as literature on the making of drugs, a pill press, scales and a shrink-wrap machine. There was evidence too that he was a member of the Royal Society of Chemistry. Other raids turned up a variety of weapons although there was no evidence that these were related to drug smuggling activities. A search of the Ferrari-driving Sean Clarke's council house turned up £50,000 in cash – not bad for a man earning only £250 a week.

A week later, Leonard Haworth was arrested on his return from Malaysia where he claimed to have been trying to sell boats to a south-east Asian government.

Certainly, Operation Humble was well organized by customs and the police, because they too had had time to plan the operation. They had had early warnings that something was being planned and had for ten months maintained surveillance on Rothermel and the others. Undercover officers had shadowed all of them at meetings at different times. They had watched to see how various beaches were visited and assessed and had been able to forecast precisely when and where the attempt to land the drugs would take place. On one occasion customs officers had followed Rothermel and a lady friend to Calais for a secret meeting with Sean Clarke.

In the end, after hearing this quite fascinating tale of cat and mouse, one story of intelligent planning overtaken by another of yet more intelligent planning, the jury found the eight men guilty. Both women were found innocent of all charges. Mark Rothermel was given five years. Clarke was sentenced to four years, and Angel Jiminez and Bryan Richardson to three and a half. Haworth also received three and a half years, but a further 18 months was added for an outstanding offence. The others, Clements, Howes and McCann, were all sentenced to three years.

Rothermel is without doubt a villain but he is one of the more interesting of his breed. He is, unlike so many others in these pages, a first-generation crook. His choice to live and work in the underworld must seem a mystery to those who know his family background. To the criminals among whom he has chosen to work, he seems to be regarded as an eccentric, an exotic, but he is not a misfit in either of the worlds he inhabits. He appears to be a man at home across the social spectrum. Rothermel has been dubbed 'The Colonel'. According to some, the reason for this is that he plans with military precision but it also suggests to others a kind of affectionate mocking of a man the criminal world admires and has taken as one of their own.

WHEN PIGLET
MET ALEKSEI

---❀---

On or about 9th March 2002 Piglet contacted the Russian Embassy in London offering to sell them top military secrets. He left a contact number and within a day received a response. The Russians were interested, the heavily accented Aleksei told him. Could they meet? They could, Piglet told the Russian, and they fixed a date. But spies cannot be too careful. 'Let's meet in London,' Piglet said, anxious to propose somewhere anonymous, somewhere cosmopolitan. Clearly he had been thinking about the arrangements for the meeting – at an appointed time, Aleksei was to wait by a particular telephone box outside Holborn tube station. He would be called there. Perhaps, Aleksei suggested, Piglet could bring a sample of his wares. Of course he could. This was real cloak-and-dagger stuff, right out of a John le Carré novel.

Aleksei turned up at the rendezvous on time and awaited the call. When it came he was told to go to Temple station, and there Piglet identified himself. The pair then took a taxi to the Crest Hotel at Tower Bridge. No one would be surprised to see a foreigner talking to an Englishman there. The two men settled down to talk in the hotel. Perhaps if anyone took any notice of them they would dismiss them as two businessmen or salesmen discussing a deal in earnest, hushed tones. Well, it was certainly a deal they were discussing. Had he brought anything worthwhile, the Russian asked Piglet. Certainly, he had. He had brought along some CDs which contained full details of Halo (Hostile Artillery Locater), a battlefield device developed by BAe Systems which enabled the recording and analysis of the sound of incoming artillery shells. From such information computers could work out the precise location of enemy fire. Aleksei was pleased; this was significant material, worth much to his country. And worth much to Piglet too. Would there be anything more, Piglet was asked. Yes, most certainly, within days. He could offer seven packages of material: four at £25,000 each and three at £10,000. It was really important stuff, some on disk, some photocopied documents, but quality stuff. Aleksei would be even more pleased with this, Piglet assured him. They arranged a second meeting for Friday, 22nd March. They would meet at the Esplanade pub at Southend. The two men parted, both highly satisfied at the way in which their meeting had gone. Aleksei was off to wherever he lived in London and Piglet went back to his modest semi in Rochford.

Rochford? Do spies really live in places like Rochford? And are they really like Piglet? They shouldn't be, not really; they oughtn't to be ordinary, humdrum chaps like him. We know what spies are like. We ought to because we've seen them often enough at the cinema or on the telly, and they aren't like Piglet. They aren't the sort of men who act as publicity secretary for the Rochford and Castle Point Ramblers Association. They don't organize weekend walks through the countryside. That's just not their style, surely. They aren't keep-fit fanatics or amateur artists. They haven't been married for 18 years, with two teenage boys who are universally praised for their politeness. Of course, it might all be just a long-cultivated deep cover. Piglet might have fooled people for years. Perhaps Richard Paternoster, the rambling club chairman, had been tricked. 'He is the last person you would expect to have anything to do with spying,' Paternoster told the press. 'He is just a family man who enjoys getting out and about in the country.' Perhaps the neighbours who described Piglet and his family so warmly had been deceived by an apparently chatty, decent man who planned to betray his country. Do spies really take their children and their friends swimming? Are they usually regarded as friendly, humorous men? Don't they normally keep themselves separate; aren't they men who have lives that they do not wish others to share?

But Piglet, better known as Ian Parr, was the least likely of spies. Or rather he does not fit our stereotypical views of what spies ought to be like. Parr was one of 1,300 employees at BAe Systems

Avionics at Basildon. He had worked there for 15 years. The firm, formerly known as British Aerospace, is one of the United Kingdom's leading suppliers of civil and military electronic systems. The factory at Basildon is involved in the research, development and manufacture of a range of sensitive defence equipment. It makes military communications equipment, weapons guidance systems and thermal imaging cameras. It is one of Europe's leading suppliers of civil and military electronic systems for air, land and sea. Its products include systems for the Tornado and Sea Harrier jets. Other products include digital terrain navigation systems, helmet mounted displays and sights, target and detection systems, night bombing equipment, autotracking systems and night vision goggles. In short, this factory is a major source of this country's weaponry. And here Ian Parr worked, in charge of a team responsible for designing microchips and making circuit boards for many of these key weapons systems. Were his colleagues surprised when they learnt that he was a spy? Looking back over the years did they now recognize the signs that he would betray his country's security for money? Not at all. They had liked him. He was a good workmate, a 'jolly and outgoing' man. They were astounded to learn that he was being charged with espionage, with obtaining information 'prejudicial to the safety or interests of the state', that he had attempted to sell information which was 'calculated to be, or might be, directly or indirectly useful to an enemy'. Whoever would have thought it? Ian Parr, a spy.

But you just can't trust the Russians. A perfectly sincere English chap gets in touch with them – rings the Russian Embassy and offers them some prime secret information about the latest weaponry – and what do they do? They get in contact with MI5. You can't even trust them to act like proper spies. No, they just shrug their shoulders, ring their opposite numbers and say, 'By the way, one of your lads has been trying to sell us some of your latest military developments. Do you want his name?' And that's just how it was with Ian Parr. At least, that's one version of what occurred. Or was it that the Russians believed they were being set up by British Intelligence and were getting out of some perceived trap in the only way they could? Or was it that ultimately they instinctively had little faith in the competence of the man who had approached them and who had given himself the code name Piglet?

In any event within hours of that initial approach to the Russians, MI5 were aware of what Parr was up to. Operation Dragonfly, a joint intelligence service and Essex police venture, was under way, and Aleksei – or rather the G Branch agent who called himself by that name, a man who could produce a most convincing Russian accent – was fitting in with Piglets' rather elaborate arrangements for their first meeting.

After the Crest Hotel meeting, Aleksei returned to his department with the startling news that Piglet was offering to provide details of a number of projects. In his summer house he had hidden disks and documents representing millions of pounds worth of research and development costs. These included Storm Shadow, the air-launched stealth cruise missile which was being rushed into service to give RAF fighter jets patrolling no-fly zones over Iraq greater high-precision targeting.

As for Parr, unaware of how the Russians had responded to his offer, he thought it was all going ahead smoothly and that shortly his bank balance would improve. He had been worried for some time about the prospect of redundancy. Now his immediate financial anxieties at least were over. At work he went about his tasks in his usual responsible manner. It was odd, though, that he had found it relatively easy to make copies over several days of so much classified material, just because he had security clearance on account of his good character. Perhaps it now crossed his mind that he might have started on this game at an earlier stage. Even so there might still be opportunities for similar trading before BAe got rid of him. He had already taken much good stuff. In addition to Storm Shadow, there was information on the new navigation system for the F16 bomber and a thermal imaging and radio jamming system. And there could be more.

And so to Southend, to the Esplanade pub on 22nd March, Aleksei with his secret smiles and Piglet with his plastic bag containing 56 floppy disks and fourteen sets of documents. Aleksei hands over a first instalment of £25,000 and Piglet in turn gives him all the material he has brought with him. Aleksei says

The Esplanade pub where Piglet met Aleksei. (Robert Hallmann)

it's time for him to be off; it's not wise to make oneself too obvious. No, he won't have a drink. He leaves with his plastic bag of goodies. But Piglet intends to celebrate, even if he is on his own. A lager, he tells the barman. He'll enjoy this. He'll toast himself and his great good luck. Only a fortnight earlier he took the risk, hesitatingly telephoned the Russians, and here he was now with so much money and the balance still to come. At this point the accounts tend to differ. Some say that he never even started on the lager. Others suggest that he'd nearly finished it. No matter; the important thing is that he had little time to enjoy his drink, for the police now came in and he was arrested.

Twenty police officers searched Parr's Rochford home in front of his astounded family and the awed attention of the neighbourhood. There were numerous other documents in the house, all of them highly marketable. In the succeeding days Ian

Parr was charged with nine offences alleging that he obtained 'documents and information prejudicial to the interest of the State which were intended to be passed on to the enemy'. The nine offences related to six counts of allegedly obtaining commercially sensitive documents and material, and three of communicating that material on two separate occasions. Each of the offences carried a maximum sentence of 14 years' imprisonment.

How the tabloids loved this case, concentrating not on the fall of a hitherto seemingly responsible man but upon his career in the army in the 1970s. The *Sun*, the *Mirror* and the other popular tabloids sought out Parr's former military colleagues. It was apparently not an auspicious career. Parr was described by some of his former army chums as 'Hazard, a one-man calamity zone'. During his service with the Lancers he had not inspired confidence. He was, one said, a 'cack handed' gunner-operator on Scorpion light tanks. Where Parr was there were always accidents, and he was as often as not bandaged as a consequence of his clumsiness. Some recalled that he had overloaded and blown up the washing machine in the barracks. Others recalled that he had injured himself loading shells into a gun turret. He was, they said, a liability.

It seems that Parr was not a typical military man. He had different interests. He wasn't a great beer drinker; he preferred wine. He wasn't one to chase after the girls. He went off rambling. He was certainly different and perhaps that has coloured some of his former colleagues' perceptions of him. After all, as a civilian he had won golden opinions from his bosses and workmates and from his neighbours. But in the period leading up to and during the trial he was scorned by the tabloids. The *Daily Mirror* wrote of him: 'He's definitely not James Bond – nor even Austin Powers. But now the world's worst spy, codenamed Piglet, is facing 14 years in jail after bungling an attempt to sell secrets to the Russians.' And there was no attempt to keep secret the fact that in Belmarsh, awaiting trial, he attempted suicide by wiring his spectacles to the main but only succeeded in burning his face. This was another example of 'Hazard' living up to his reputation, the tabloids shouted gleefully. How typical that the man should devise such a half-baked plot to sell military secrets.

At the Old Bailey trial in April 2003, the prosecutors, Sally Walsh and Aftab Jafferjee, accepted that Parr 'a long-standing employee of British Aerospace ... has acknowledged he abused his position of trust'. But despite his failure, the enormity of what he had tried to do could not be ignored. Most of the material he stole was rated either 'UK restricted' or 'NATO restricted', admittedly relatively low in the hierarchy of classified material, but at the same time it was all subject to section 1 of the Official Secrets Act of 1911. In particular, Storm Shadow was of such a sensitive nature that the trial judge, the Recorder of London, Mr Justice Hyam, was given details in a separate folder that the rest of the court was not privileged to see. According to defence experts, Storm Shadow was the greatest single improvement in modern times to the RAF's capacity to attack an enemy. The Russians would have been delighted to have details of its unique capabilities. Doubtless such information would have led to the development of counter-measures. That no details of any of the projects fell into the hands of other agencies was not to lessen Parr's blame. By his actions he could have compromised the effectiveness of British fighter planes in Iraq, the prosecution told the Old Bailey.

Rock Tansey, QC, could present only a very thin case for his client. He had been, said Mr Tansey, 'a model citizen, a very good neighbour, an excellent employee, and a devoted husband and father. His actions were totally out of character and totally inexplicable to his family and friends, and almost inexplicable to himself'. Parr was a former soldier and 'the last thing he would do or seek to do or intend to do would be to harm this country'. There was a feeble attempt by Parr to claim that he knew all the time that Aleksei was a British agent and that he handed over the documents only to play along. But that version is nonsense. The story does not hang together. Sentencing Parr to ten years – eight for contravening the Official Secrets Act and two for stealing the documents – the judge told him, 'You knew perfectly well the nature of what you were doing. I do not and cannot accept that you did not appreciate that what you were doing was a risk to national security.'

So was this man a villain? Was he a traitor? Did he endanger the security of the country and its servicemen? Was the possibility of redundancy behind his ridiculous plot? Did he regard what he was doing simply as industrial espionage? He must have been aware of the significance of the material he was trying to sell. After the trial Detective Supt Gareth Wilson of Essex police said: 'As a former soldier he was more than aware of the potential consequence of his actions.' It is difficult not to concur with that conclusion.

Parr had tried to tell the police that it was a moment of madness to strike out at his employers, to get back at them for his possible redundancy. He had, as his wife said, 'always put 100 per cent into everything. He put everything into his work'. Perhaps it was the sense that BAe was betraying him that led him to his act of treachery. Perhaps if there had never been a mention of redundancy he would have continued as a loyal servant of the company.

It is ironic then that his fears of redundancy were misplaced. On the day before his arrest he had been recommended for a £1,000 per annum rise. BAe had recognized a first-class employee.

RIGHT AND WRONG

———— ✿ ————

Scene: One of several pubs in urban Essex.
Time: Any Sunday lunchtime in the past 20 years

It's the day of the traditional drink-up, the day to talk about yesterday's football match, or perhaps not so much about the match as about the fighting. Or possibly they're talking about last week's shindy with the Anti-Nazi League, swopping tales of individual heroism, warrior tales, about one man booted, another glassed, yet another with his head smashed open with an iron bar, and an Asian shopkeeper and his family terrified. These men, they're a warrior caste. They're men apart, shaven headed, heavily tattooed, and they fight for a way of life that is being destroyed. Do you remember the abandoned international football match at Lansdowne Road, Dublin, in 1995? They were the boys who stopped that game, brought it to a halt, caused a riot. They let people know they were there; they let the IRA know they were there. They taught them a lesson. These men, they're the last guardians of the English and their standards, and they see it all crumbling round them – the traitors in the Labour party as well as the Tories letting it all go to the dogs, letting the Reds run the show, and the Jews, and the gays, and the niggers, with no thought for the English, the true race, the great race, the Aryans. They fight hard. They're not afraid. They're out on the street making their point, fighting for us. The country, the world, it's all going down the drain, they say, and they're going to fight, going to turn things round.

'Eventually there will be a race war,' they say, 'and we have to be strong enough in numbers to win. We'll die to keep this country pure and if it means bloodshed at the end of the day, then let it be.' It's all so simple, no arguing about it. 'White Revolution is the only solution.' They tell us that there is no moral leadership any more. 'The Church of England is now so full of poofs and every sort of scum, what can you expect?'

This is how it's done, this race war, this ethnic cleansing. On Europe's largest housing estate, Harold Hill in Romford, an Asian family was subjected to two months of attacks and harassment until they were forced to leave. Steve Sargent, a major propagandist for Combat 18, seemed to dismiss the idea that anything very serious had occurred. 'I only heard that the family dog was thrown through the front window dead,' he said. Ethnic cleansing – in Africa, in Kosovo, in Ireland, in Harold Hill.

These men are Holocaust deniers. To them it never happened; it's a lie, a Jewish lie, a Leftie lie. So when some of them are in Poland for an England football match they take time out to visit Sachsenhausen, the site of the former concentration camp. It's time for a laugh. To them it's a place for Nazi salutes, a place to vandalize the museum, to lie on the slabs used by Nazi scientists to carry out experiments, to pose in the ovens. 'Next time,' says their magazine, commemorating this trip, 'we're gonna incinerate every last stinking one of 'em! No Fuss! No Mess! Just pure cyanide!'

This then is an introduction to Combat 18. Its members are on the far-right, extremists whose method is violence. They are still at work but their most active days were during the five years from 1992. At first they had acted as heavies for the British National Party, protecting them at their meetings, but the BNP was too respectable in the eyes of some, what with their ideas of standing for election; that would never work. So Combat 18 became a group in its own right. They had no time for elections. The only way to gain respect was as a paramilitary group, Charlie Sargent told his followers in 1996. And note that title – 'Combat' well, that's obvious enough, but 18? That figure represents the first and eighth letters of the alphabet – A and H – Adolf and Hitler. But let it not be thought that there is for the majority of the members any coherent political philosophy behind the outpourings of hatred and venom. For most, Combat 18 provides no more than an excuse for mayhem.

The leaders of the newly formed movement were the Sargent brothers, Charlie and Steve, living at that time in a flat in Cornflower Road in Chelmsford. The brothers, both plasterers by trade, were active Arsenal supporters when young, ardent skinheads, earning their first serious scars in post-match street fighting. Charlie is said to have bitten off somebody's nose in a fight. One of his three terms of imprisonment was for wounding a man with an axe. He had convictions for drugs and for the possession of a gun. A dangerous man, he regularly carried a knife. He finally found his niche as a warrior of the far-right. And when he addressed his followers, readied them for the fray, choruses of Sieg Heils echoed back as the arms were raised in Nazi salutes. 'Our Race is Our Nation,' was the slogan. Steve Sargent had won equal fame as a street fighter, against other football supporters and against those he deemed enemies of England. More intelligent than his brother, he became editor of the Combat 18 magazine and organized the sale of T-shirts, concerts by neo-Nazi bands, and their compact discs.

But the other and perhaps more significant leader of Combat 18 was the ferociously aggressive Will Browning, 'The Beast', who had served a three year sentence for attacking some black youths. An even more violent man than the Sargents, he nevertheless had some standards in his warped view of the world. He had a puritanical quality missing from so many in Combat 18. Where the others indulged themselves with excessive drinking, he was moderate. He was against pornography and strip clubs. But he was serious in wishing to overturn the liberal society which he believed to be destroying the country. His proposed methods were radical. He had published instructions on how to make home-made bombs and under lists and addresses of those he thought were left-wing activists he wrote 'Kill 'em all.'

From instructions like this came the threats to people in the public eye, among them Paddy Ashdown, Anna Ford, Sharron Davies (who is married to a black athlete), Vanessa Redgrave, Graham Norton, and Bernard Levin. The lay preacher, Lynette Bruno, the mother of the boxer, was told to 'go home and die'. Colin Jarrett, the black athlete, had his home fire-bombed.

In *Redwatch* Browning reminds Combat 18 members of their aims: 'To ship all non-whites back to Africa, Asia, Arabia, or in body bags ... To execute all queers ... To execute all white race mixers ... To weed out all Jews in the Government, the media, the arts, the professions ... To execute all Jews who have actively helped to damage the white race and to put into camps the rest until we find a solution for the eternal Jew.'

But in the meantime what could be done? A few, a very few, like the Sargents' idea of a Homeland. It's not for Jews or foreigners, this Homeland. It's for the dispossessed English, squeezed out of their homes by the tide of immigration. And the Homeland will be in Essex, an area with relatively cheap housing and yet close to London. Here Combat 18 will take over white estates; here they will enlist discontented young men to join the sacred cause. At first Chelmsford will be the power base from which to begin the resistance. Later, Witham will become the Aryan centre. It will be an almost independent state, cleansed of all seen as aliens. It will be a no-go area for non-Aryans. Members of the new society will separate themselves from the degenerate society they despise.

Only a few, though, really believe in the idea of a Homeland. Most can't take it seriously. They can't just uproot themselves from the places they know. How will they live? Where will they work? Do their wives and families want to come to some place called the Homeland? Most are there for the fighting, for the buzz; so in the end the idea simply fades away. But it was a murder which led to the eventual demise of Combat 18. And it all came about because of the music, their neo-Nazi music and its neo-Nazi lyrics.

Blood and Honour, an established fascist music company which organized concerts and merchandising for a number of right-wing bands, had been taken over by the Sargents, who ran the mail order side. Will Browning, who sang with No Remorse, produced discs under his own ISD label, with lyrics containing extreme material. Large crowds attended secret gigs to listen to skinhead bands such as Skrewdriver, Celtic Warrior, English Rose, Chingford Attack (from the Waltham Forest area) and Battlezone (from Chelmsford). There were many well-attended gigs in Essex. Blood and Honour's compact discs and other merchandise were sold illegally all over the world. Those far-right bands which did not fall in under Combat 18's banner were mercilessly beaten.

Such bands might have shared the same views on race, but the commercial instincts of the Sargents and Browning were extremely acute, overcoming any shared philosophical beliefs. Huge amounts of cash began to pour into the coffers. Between 1994 and 1997, ISD made an estimated profit of between £100,000 and £200,000. Browning spent none of this on himself. He was using it to promote the race war.

The music and the lyrics carried the same message as all of the propaganda leaflets, the street chants and Charlie's rabble-rousing speeches. In whatever venue they played, the songs were spat out, gobbets of racial hate. One typical song, entitled 'The Niggers Came Over' contains the lines

> 'Shoot the niggers! The Pakis too!
> Hang the Reds and we'll gas the Jews.
> If you're black you're going back
> With a bit of luck in a body bag.'

Then there came a split in Combat 18, right at the top, between Browning and Charlie Sargent, who had established the National Socialist Alliance, an umbrella network for many extremist right-wing groups, all aiming to overthrow 'the system'. This poisoned the relationship between Sargent and Browning. There was also the problem of the music. Much of the profit was going to Browning's ISD label. Charlie was furious. The cash ought to be coming to Combat 18 and to the National Socialist Alliance. But he could not get the accounts from Browning. For his part Browning was furious that Charlie was worrying more about the CDs than engaging in serious terrorism. While Browning was initiating a letter-bomb campaign with Danish neo-Nazis, Charlie Sargent was spending too much time on his profitable sidelines, selling shirts and CDs. In any case, Browning argued that Charlie owed him money. There was Charlie Sargent, unemployed, but wearing fancy designer clothing and always with money to spend on beer. The puritanical Browning felt that Charlie Sargent was no true revolutionary. The two men were drifting further apart.

Browning then claimed that the Sargents had been expelled from Combat 18 for trying to divide the movement. Both men

Charlie Sargent attending a far-right rally. (Courtesy of David Hoffman Photo Library)

canvassed support. Charlie Sargent was said to have threatened that he would knife Browning when he met him. Hearing of this, Browning left a message on Charlie's answerphone challenging him to a fight. A second message warned that if Charlie was not careful he would find himself face-down in a ditch. So these opponents of the degenerate society faced up to each other.

In January 1997 Browning and two others went to the mobile home at Sherrards House, Harlow, where Charlie's partner, Maxine, lived as a single parent with their children. As Charlie was not there on this occasion, the three men went on to Chelmsford to look for Steve Sargent. He was absent too and so his front door was kicked in and the flat searched. Weeks later, on Monday, 10th February, Browning and Chris Castle, a Combat 18 member from Catford, returned to the Harlow mobile home park. There are conflicting views of what really did occur but there is no doubt that Castle died from a single stab wound in the back. Charlie Sargent and Martin Cross were charged with murder. Their trial took place at Chelmsford Crown Court in January 1998.

While the prosecution claimed that it was a case of premeditated murder, the defence case argued that Cross was defending himself and Sargent from attack. Browning told the court that they had gone to meet Charlie by arrangement. They had with them Charlie's plastering tools, which they had been withholding from him for some weeks. It had been agreed that they would be returned to him provided that Charlie handed over the subscription lists for both Blood and Honour and Combat 18. In addition they claimed that he owed them £1,000. According to Browning, he left the car park and strolled up the main road, believing that if he met Charlie negotiations would break down. It was Chris Castle who went to the door of the mobile home. Shortly afterwards, returning to the car park, Browning saw Castle staggering, his hand to his chest. He thought he had been hit and winded. Then, as Castle collapsed to the ground, Sargent and Cross came on the scene. Sargent was carrying a crossbow, Browning said, and Cross had a knife in his hand. Browning saw blood on Castle's back.

'What the f*** have you done? Go and get a f*** ambulance or he'll die.'

'F*** him,' Sargent answered. 'Let him rot.'

'He's a casualty of war,' Cross told him.

Unable to find his car keys, Browning struggled with Castle to the road and managed to call a taxi. They went to the nearest hospital but Castle was dead on arrival. He had been stabbed once in the back.

At the trial the defence set out to prove that Browning was a man to be feared, a psychopath of whom the defendants were afraid. Hadn't Browning served three years in 1989 for violence? Didn't he carry a gun? Hadn't he carried one in a Mile End pub the previous year? Hadn't he once in Chelmsford walked round with a gun stuck in his waistband? Didn't he carry a rifle in his car boot? Weren't there books and magazines about guns and bomb-making in his house? The jury saw a video of a 1995 *World in Action* programme when Browning attacked the camera crew with a screwdriver. Hadn't he also threatened to kill Sargent at two skinhead gigs where he had been seen carrying a crowbar and possibly a hammer? And at the Harlow mobile home, so the court was asked, hadn't Browning and Castle been the aggressors?

A prosecution witness called Vogel gave further graphic testimony about the easy acceptance of violence in the world of the far-right. He told how he and other Combat 18 members were in a pub in Gallywood, Chelmsford, on the Saturday before the murder. He told how Sargent said he would deal with Browning and how he began recruiting people to take on his rival. The following weekend Vogel was in a Romford pub where he heard Sargent boasting about the killing of Castle. The defence replied that it was Browning who had made threats which had to be taken seriously.

About the actual day of the murder, no one could prove Sargent's assertion that Browning had been carrying a gun. However, there was evidence that Sargent had told a witness to tell the police that Browning was carrying a gun. Sargent's claim that he had not expected Browning or Castle to call on him was put into doubt by telephone records which seemed to confirm that he had been told to expect a visit.

Cross described how Castle was stabbed.

'I was standing in the kitchen and the kids and my wife and Maxine were in the living room. Just like out the blue, I heard a bang and there was a commotion, and the kids were screaming and my wife was screaming. This all happened in seconds. Then I saw an altercation, people beating up on Charlie and I recognized these people. I knew them instantly. It was an irrational situation, but I knew because of who these people were, these people had come to kill Charlie and me. In that instant I picked up a knife from the kitchen and, er ... it was all – it all happened in seconds

'– and I lunged towards one of the people, and then that person and the other person that was there, they ran off.' The simple self-defence of a frightened man, protecting his friend who had been intimidated by Browning for weeks.

Under oath Charlie confirmed that in the car park Browning had pointed a gun at him. 'He said he was going to kill me. I could see this little gun and a bag.' It was only then, Charlie said, that he realized Castle had been stabbed.

There were so many discrepancies between the accounts offered to the court and the police. Even the statements offered by Charlie Sargent and Cross were sometimes at variance. In the end the jury teased out the details to arrive at what does seem to be the nearest to the truth that can be ascertained, and found Sargent and Cross guilty of premeditated murder. Both received life sentences.

Browning, whose supporters had maintained a menacing presence in the public gallery and outside the courtroom during the trial, was a hero. Recently released from a short prison sentence on racist charges, he was there to watch Sargent in the dock. And now he was the undisputed leader of Combat 18. But Combat 18, the majority of whose followers were there principally for the thrill of fighting – many operated under the banner of the Chelsea Headhunters and others were Millwall and West Ham supporters – had lost its strength, and its numbers dwindled. Some tired of violence and settled down to work and families; some joined other groups; and some gave up altogether because they heard that Charlie Sargent had really been an agent of MI5. Charlie, it was whispered, had been selling them down the river all the time. The business of supporting the paramilitary groups in Northern

The logo used by Combat 18.

Ireland, marching with the Apprentice Boys in Belfast, smuggling arms into Ulster, was nothing but a ruse. It was all part of the British security forces' strategy to infiltrate the Ulster Defence Force and other loyalist groups. Or so it was said. Of course, that might have just been a ploy by MI5, to confuse and sow dissension. It certainly did little good for Combat 18.

However, even if Combat 18 has faded, it is not dead, and still the same old theories are heard and the same old solutions are proposed. In 2001 Browning appeared at Southwark Crown Court on charges of inciting violence at the Bloody Sunday memorial rally. He received 80 hours' community service. In February 2004 there were reports that prominent Jews were being targeted with hate-mail and graffiti attacks on their homes. Uri Geller had the word 'Jew' paint-sprayed on his garden fence as though the word itself was an insult. Barbara Roche, a former Home Office minister, Lord Triesman, a former general secretary of the Labour Party, and others were similarly treated. And Combat 18 was being held responsible.

Combat 18 has not gone away.

LINE-UPS

———————— ✦ ————————

It was two o'clock in the morning, Sunday, 5th November 1972, and the band was still playing at the Barn Restaurant. Just shows you what a thriving place it had become. Only a few years earlier it had been a little roadside café, but under the energetic ownership of Bob Patience and the wholehearted contributions of his wife and his son and daughter, all of whom worked there, the place had become a much sought after spot for a meal and evening entertainment. It wasn't just people from Braintree who patronized it now. People even came out from London. That's the kind of successful night-spot the low white building had become. With its beamed ceiling and the horse brasses on the walls and the low-hanging oil lamps above each table, you might have thought it a real old-fashioned country sort of place; at least, you might have thought that if you'd spent most of your days in town.

With the band still playing and the dancers seemingly tireless, Muriel Patience and her daughter, Beverley, decided to call it a night and set off for Sun Lido House, their home, only 50 yards away from the restaurant. David and his father, Bob, would stay, on not expecting to finish much before four o'clock. The two women stepped through the front door and into the hall. They went into the darkened kitchen and it was there that they had their first shock. There were two men waiting there. One of them, in a raincoat, waved a gun. They were told that if they kept quiet nothing would happen to them. They were bustled into the sitting room. By now Muriel Patience was in tears, already shaking with fright. 'Keep quiet,' the gunman told her. 'It won't make a noise if I have to use it,' he told her, nodding at the gun. In his other hand he carried a cushion, which he placed over the muzzle of the gun. It would make an effective silencer.

It was the safe keys they wanted. Where was the boss, and when was he coming back to the house, they asked. When did they expect him? Frightened though they were, the women did not divulge the keys' whereabouts. They were probably over in the restaurant, they said, though they knew that they were in a vase on the mantelpiece. Muriel, between bouts of tears, was bitter. 'You work hard all your life and then someone like you takes it away,' she said.

Twenty minutes later Bob Patience strolled over to the house and straight into the sitting room. And there sat the gunman and his companion. And there on the settee was Beverley with her arms round her mother, trying to comfort her. Before he had time to ask any questions, he was told to sit down. The safe keys, where were they? In his statement Bob said, 'I did not panic. I looked the gunman straight in the eye. It was a game of bluff. I was playing for time because I knew I would be missed by my staff.' What exactly was said is unclear but Bob was using his sharp businessman's brain to outwit them.

There was a period of perhaps half an hour when it seems that Bob Patience's strategy worked. There were threats and demands but as yet no offer of violence. At one point, Beverley asked the gunman if he really thought that they could get away with it. He answered, 'This is so well planned it cannot go wrong.' The second man, the taller of the two, said little, though he came out with one memorable phrase. 'I only do as I'm told,' he said.

Neither of the intruders was masked. Both were becoming increasingly uneasy at the way in which the family held out against their demands. Perhaps what followed gives an indication of the desperation that they must now be feeling. The man with the gun was increasingly angry. He wanted the job over and done with now. They had been there too long already.

The statements of Bob and Beverley Patience describe what finally occurred. There was another demand for the keys. The gunman said, 'You had better have them, Bob.' He aimed the gun at the women. 'Your wife or your daughter?' he asked and the gun went from one woman to the other. He paused. 'Your wife, I think,' he said and then for a few seconds was silent, the gun pointing at Muriel. Was this another threat? Why take it out on poor Muriel, who was more distressed than her husband and daughter? The gunman held the cushion to her head. Could he really mean it? 'He ... raised his gun and shot her through the right temple ... My wife was in a terrible state with blood from her wound and blood from her mouth. She rolled off the settee in agony.' Beverley knelt down to help her mother. There was a hole above her right eye. Bob jumped up, 'You have shot my wife, you bastard,' he shouted. The gunman went over to Muriel and leaned over her. 'She'll be all right,' he said dismissively. It was only a graze, he said. He repeated his demand for the keys. Bob Patience could argue no longer. He took them from the vase, went over to the safe, and handed over two money bags containing about £900.

Then Bob and Beverley were made to lie face down on the floor and were tied up. Muriel was groaning and weeping, the blood running down her face. Would they telephone for an ambulance? 'She's not dying,' the gunman told them.

Now the gunman knelt on Beverley's back and bending down with the cushion, he fired into her back. One cry and she was silent. Then the gunman turned to Bob.

The cushion was placed on his head. He heard the deafening report. And then the two men left the house. It had been nothing more than an execution.

Mercifully it was a badly carried out execution. Bob Patience, who had not expected to live, almost immediately struggled to his feet, staggered to the telephone and called his son David in the restaurant, urging him to call an ambulance. David made the call and then went to the house. He saw his own Volkswagen being driven across the car park. As it sped past he had only the slightest glimpse of the man in the passenger seat.

All three were taken to hospital. The bullet had passed through Beverley's back and exited through her chest, missing the main artery of the heart by a quarter of an inch. Bob Patience was even more fortunate. He had moved his head at the moment the shot was fired and escaped with a slight wound to the ear. But Muriel was unconscious.

Bob was able to give the police a description of the two men. One of them, the gunman, he described as slim, about 5ft 8in tall, with short sandy hair. He was thin faced and sallow with very blue eyes. He spoke with a northern accent. He was, Patience estimated, in his early thirties. Although it was not publicised, the man was also said to have a lazy eye.

The second man, in his late twenties, was 6 ft tall, slim and broad shouldered. He had a thin face and brown eyes. With such clear descriptions and with the recovery of the bullets, the police were hopeful of an early arrest.

On 8th November photofit pictures of the men were released to television and newspapers. Bob Patience offered a substantial reward but there was no immediate response although there was the inevitable public outrage when the news came that Muriel Patience had died. Still unconscious, she had lingered three days in Braintree hospital before dying. On 10th November, Beverley added further details about the men's appearance from her bed in the intensive care unit and a second photofit was published. In the meantime, the car was found abandoned several miles from Braintree.

Then came a lead. It was an underworld whisper. George Ince, a man with a record of shop-breaking and a reputation for brawling, might be worth looking at. But where was he? – certainly not in his usual haunts. He had just disappeared. There was no sign of him. Then, quite out of the blue, he turned up with his legal representative at Epping police station. He had read that the police wanted to speak to him. Well, here he was. But was he really likely? He was 5ft 10ins tall, did not have a lazy eye, did not have sandy hair, and did not have a Yorkshire accent.

On 27th November Ince appeared at a number of identity parades at Colchester police station. He was identified by Bob and Beverley as the unmasked gunman; by David Patience as the passenger in the stolen car; by two others who said that they had seen him in the district when he might have been planning the robbery.

On 2nd May 1973 the trial opened at Chelmsford before Mr Justice Melford Stevenson. George Ince was charged with the murder of Muriel Patience; with the attempted murder of Bob and Beverley Patience, with wounding both of them, and with intent to do grievous harm to both. A further charge related to the theft of credit slips for about £900.

The prosecution presented five identity witnesses. The two least important were Bernard Laysell, a lorry driver, who said that he had seen Ince with another man in the Chequers pub at Felsted on 2nd November, three days before the murder. He had felt so uneasy about the men that he had written down their car number. Whilst the car number was not found to be connected to Ince, Laysell had no doubt that he had correctly identified him at the line-up. A 16-year-old schoolboy, James Faulkner, also identified Ince as a man he had seen in a newspaper shop in Felsted on 2nd November. But this was all very inconclusive.

David Patience told the court how he had seen the two men in his car. At the Colchester identity parade on 27th November, he picked out Ince as the passenger. But even he might have seemed an unconvincing witness, for he admitted to having seen the car's occupant for no more than three seconds.

But the testimony of Bob and Beverley Patience was telling. They had sat with the gunman and his accomplice for over half an hour. Surely they could not fail to recognise the man in the dock. In court, Bob recognised Ince as the gunman. Even so, he had not initially identified Ince in the line-up. He had stood in front of him for several seconds before pointing to another man. He had gone away and then realised that he had made an error. He returned to the line-up and this time selected Ince. There was an untidiness about this and perhaps some members of the jury might have had some doubts. Beverley who had identified Ince as the gunman on 27th November also recognised him in the courtroom. It was during her testimony that Ince stood up, creating a disturbance and shouting, 'Why don't you tell the truth?' Beverley broke down in tears, Ince was ordered out of the court, and proceedings were adjourned for 20 minutes. On resumption, Ince announced, 'I would like to apologise to the court, sir. But I'm not the man who done it.'

However, Ince was not a man to restrain himself. He peremptorily sacked Victor Durand, his counsel. This was a point of principle rather than any dissatisfaction with the defence team. He was really dissatisfied with the attitude of Mr Justice Melford

Stevenson who, he said, was biased and rude. During one recess Ince had sent a telegram to the Lord Chancellor asking to be tried in another court and with a different judge. Ince, now without counsel, offered no defence but he asked whether he could take a truth drug. This was refused. He was asked if he would like defence counsel reinstated. No, he would not. His argument, he said, was not with counsel but with the judge. 'I am an Englishman, born in England and I want an English trial. This is not an English trial.' Victor Durand, though already dismissed by Ince, told the judge that his former client did not wish to take any further part in the trial and that he wished to go downstairs and remain there. But when Ince tried to leave the courtroom, he was told to sit down and had to be physically restrained. For the rest of the trial he stood in the dock with his back to the judge, still occasionally interrupting prosecution witnesses.

The jury retired but after nearly four hours sent a note to the judge. 'We are finding it very difficult to conclude in view of there being no defence.' Whilst the judge had hoped for a unanimous verdict, this was now clearly unlikely. He would accept a majority verdict of 10–2, he said, but 9–3 was unacceptable. From that sticking point nothing emerged and a new trial was ordered.

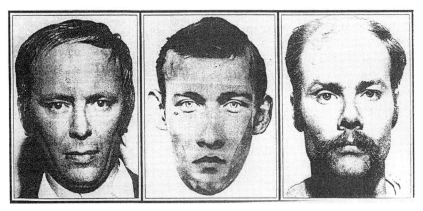

George Ince.   *The photofit.*   *John Brook.*

The following week, on Monday 15th May, the second trial began at Chelmsford before Mr Justice Eveleigh with a new jury empanelled. Ince reinstated Victor Durand as his defence counsel.

The first witness was Bob Patience, who unhesitatingly identified Ince. But it was a more combative defence now. Patience and Victor Durand clashed three times in an hour. Did he recall being shown a photograph? No, he couldn't recollect seeing a photograph. Had he seen any photographs prior to the identification parade? He didn't need to see photographs. He just needed to hear the men speak. He had asked them to say 'I want the keys to the safe'. He knew what he had heard, could remember the voice. But hadn't he described the man as having a northern accent? Ince had a pronounced Cockney accent. When invited to reconsider this Bob was adamant. 'It was the same voice as the man who shot my wife,' he said.

Beverley Patience was still in no doubt that the man in the dock had murdered her mother, but her brother David was reminded that after the Colchester line-up he had said, 'I am not 100 per cent certain but I think it could be the man.'

Bernard Laysell, who testified to having seen Ince in a Felsted pub, now said that he had identified Ince from photographs before picking him out at the line-up. And the 16-year-old James Faulkner now admitted that he could not be absolutely certain that the man in the dock was the same man he had seen in the newspaper shop.

Now came the turn of Ince to be questioned. He claimed to be completely innocent of the crime, saying that he had never been to the Barn Restaurant and had never heard of the Patience family. He had been in Whitstable on 2nd November when Laysell and Faulkner said they had seen him. On the night of the murder he had stayed with a Mrs Dorothy Gray. They had watched television until after midnight and had then gone to bed. The next morning he had returned to Whitstable.

Attention now turned to the attractive blonde, Mrs Dorothy Gray, who was called to the witness box. She said Ince had arrived at her house at about 8.45 on the evening of Saturday, 4th November, and had left the following morning at about nine o'clock. They were together in the house all that time. Then the questions became personal. Mr John Leonard QC for the prosecution had found what he believed was a weak spot, one which could sway the jury. Did Mrs Gray's husband know that she was having an affair with Ince? As far as she knew, she said, he did not know of her involvement. Yes, she was in love with Ince. Where did she first meet him? She was unsure. Possibly at a club. But she had known him for a number of years. He used to go to a billiard hall belonging to her two brothers-in-law. It was in Mile End.

Leonard: That was at the time when your husband was still about, wasn't it?

Gray: Yes.

Leonard: Your husband is not about at the moment, is he?

Gray: No.

She agreed that her husband had 'not been about' since about the middle of 1968.

Yes, she had changed her name by deed poll some time ago and her husband knew about that. How often did she meet Ince? Every Saturday night. She was just trying to give her lover an alibi, wasn't she? No, she said, she was telling the truth. 'I would like you to bear in mind the publicity I am getting. I stand to lose my home and family.' Mrs Gray was then asked when she would next see her husband. 'The following week', she replied.

Leonard: At that time he will still not be circulating in the world at large?

Gray: I suppose not.

It was rough handling of a defence witness, a ploy to discredit her, a woman who was unfaithful to her husband, a woman whose husband 'had not been about' for several years.

In his closing speech Victor Durand told how Ince had been crying out for the truth to be revealed. They had heard 'a heartfelt answer by his lover' who had suffered public degradation by her confession of adultery but they had heard her 'call of truth'. Her public disclosure increased the worth of her word a thousandfold; the defence counsel was trying to checkmate the prosecution counsel's strategy. The most that could be built up against Ince, said Durand, was that he was 'a well-bronzed layabout' who was not working. But, even if he was the most worthless creature, a man must not be convicted simply because of his character. There had been, Durand observed, a veil around 'other names, other places, billiard halls, brothers-in-law, and all the rest of it'. Whatever these signified, the jury should steel themselves against it.

And the jury did steel themselves against suspicion. Who Mrs Gray's husband was had nothing to do with Ince's guilt or innocence. What did sway the jury in the case was that they were unconvinced by the evidence of identification. They were concerned that the witnesses had all been shown photographs of men with police records prior to the line-up at Colchester on 27th November. The evidence of neither Laysell nor Faulkner was convincing nor was that of David Patience. Even Bob Patience had changed his mind at Colchester. Only Beverley had stood out, confident to the end that George Ince had murdered her mother.

When Ince was cleared to cheers and applause from the public gallery, he pointed to police officers, shouting, 'It's your turn now for the corruption.' He was led from the dock swearing, yelling, and struggling violently. But not to freedom. He was about to start a 15-year sentence for his part in the bullion robbery at Mountnessing in May 1972.

Mrs Dorothy Gray had not appeared at the first trial. Ince had feared that it might be dangerous for her to do so. Then she had courageously gone to see her husband, Charlie Kray, who was serving a 10-year sentence at Maidstone. He had been found guilty as an accessory to the murder of Jack 'The Hat' MacVitie. She had told him of her affair with Ince. She was unaware of how he might react but, surprisingly, he told her to appear as a defence witness for the man who was cuckolding him. The jury had not known when she appeared in the witness box that she had changed her name to Gray from Kray because of the bad publicity which surrounded her married name. It is impossible to gauge the effect of Mrs Gray's evidence on the jury, but the prosecution case was not strong, especially on the issue of the identification of the accused as the killer. Perhaps her evidence was not crucial to the verdict. On the other hand, had her identity been disclosed, the jury might have treated anything she said with considerably more suspicion and reserve. She was later divorced and married Ince who was allowed out of prison for the ceremony.

Reggie Kray, in his book *Born Fighter*, recalled: 'George Ince was always a slag to me, even though he used to frequent our billiard hall in the late fifties. I first tumbled that he was going with Charlie's wife, so I got hold of him outside the Double R club and butted him in the face. Ron and I then warned him off the manor of the East End and he made sure he stayed away.' Even so he did not stay away from Charlie's wife.

The mystery of the Barn murder finally began to unravel only four weeks or so after the conclusion of Ince's second trial. Police were informed that a hotel worker at Ambleside in the Lake District had been shown a gun which a fellow worker claimed had been used to kill Muriel Patience. A 30-year-old kitchen porter, recently released from Pentonville, was arrested. He most certainly matched the gunman's photofit description. John Brook was 5ft 8ins tall. He had sandy hair and a staring glass eye. And a Yorkshire accent. Furthermore, he had been boasting about the killing; gloating when Ince was on trial that 'George Ince will get me off'.

A Beretta, found sewn into his mattress, was proved by tests to be the murder weapon. Brook's acquaintances were checked and the name of Nicholas de Clare Johnson, a small-time car thief, came up. On the weekend of the murder he had been on pre-release leave from Pentonville. After his arrest, Johnson at first denied any knowledge of the murder but then he relented and made a full confession. He was not a violent man. He had met Brook when they were together in the prison psychiatric hospital. He regretted having joined up with a man he now described as a mental case. Brook had thought up the robbery and Johnson went along with the plan because he said he was afraid of him.

On trial at Chelmsford in January 1974, Johnson described how he and Brook went from Chelmsford to Braintree by bus. They waited in a field near the house until two o'clock. Johnson had thought it would be a quick job, straight in and out, a matter of minutes. He climbed into the house by an upstairs window and opened the back door to let Brook in. They searched for the safe keys. Suddenly there was a noise and the two women came in.

Johnson was shaken when he saw Brook bring a gun out of his raincoat. He had never dreamt that his companion was armed. After the shooting of Muriel Patience Johnson said that he left the house and then heard two more shots. Brook, laughing, said to him later, 'There is no witness now.' They eventually abandoned the Volkswagen and walked miles over fields before hitching a lift to Chelmsford. By the Sunday evening, his leave over, Johnson was back in Pentonville. Johnson admitted to pangs of conscience. 'I nearly came forward when George Ince was on trial,' he told the court. 'I was a coward to let another man stand trial.'

In the witness box Bob Patience came under fire from the defence. It was even suggested that he had had played some part in the Mountnessing robbery and had had some link with Ince. Beverley now admitted that she, like her father, had wrongly identified the killer. Odd, wasn't it, that a young woman and her sharp-witted businessman father should sit in the room with the gunman for at least half an hour and make such a calamitous mistake?

After a four week trial the jury reached a unanimous verdict. Brook was given life for murder and wounding plus 12 years for robbery and three years for the possession of a gun, the sentences to run concurrently. Johnson, described as having been 'harnessed to a tiger', received ten years for manslaughter and seven years for robbery, these also to run concurrently.

So how did the confusion of identity arise? Because the police had received a malicious underworld tip-off that Ince might have been involved, his picture – from 12 years before – was among those shown to the key witnesses. After inspecting the picture, Beverley told police that he had the 'right type of face', and other witnesses too had in some way responded to the photographs.

There were lessons here to be learnt: how to ensure that identity parades were properly conducted; how to be certain that adequate forensic evidence came before the court. But for two sceptical juries and a courageous witness, there would have been a serious miscarriage of justice. And had not a psychopathic killer bragged of his murder, perhaps the case might have remained unsolved.

BULL IN AN ANTIQUE SHOP

———————— ❁ ————————

It's one of those places that perhaps you drive through a couple of times or a place where you've maybe spent an hour or so on the way to somewhere else. It's the sort of little town that you promise yourself you'll come back to some day and spend a decent length of time there because it's really worth returning to. And if you don't ever manage to go back, in spite of all your intentions to do so, you still – months, perhaps even years later – have occasional glimpses of it, images which linger in the mind, if only for seconds. You see them again, the old clock tower on Market Hill, the houses' uneven roof tiles shading from red to ochre, the Great Barn, the fine church of St Peter ad Vincula, the beautifully modest houses with their painted walls of cream, palest blue, pink, or saffron, and the abbey ruins. And, of course Paycocke's, that wonderful half-timbered gem. You can imagine Coggeshall as it must have been – or as you hope it must have been – generations ago, in its heyday, populated by stout farmers and jolly clergy, by silk weavers and wool merchants.

It's a delightful little town, still prosperous, comfortable, and well-ordered, a place to settle down in, with its decent pubs, its tea rooms, and its still individual shops. Small wonder they filmed so much of the TV series *Lovejoy* here, for its highly reputable antique shops, filled with top-class, quality stuff, attract buyers from London and abroad. Their windows reveal good oak tables, delicate mahogany whatnots, china of the first order, and shining brass, just the kind of stuff the advertiser was looking for when he posted the following in *Country Life* in April 1986: 'Wilfred Bull, dealer in antiques … wishes to buy walnut or mahogany furniture for a handsome price and would welcome any invitation to call and see you'.

Wilfred Bull was not some fly-by-night dealer. He had an international reputation, and his showroom and warehouse in West Street contained one of the best stocks of fine furniture in the Home Counties. He and his wife Patsy were well-known figures at major antiques fairs and exhibitions throughout Britain and Europe and for 25 years they had lived and worked in the town. In April 1985 they were photographed with Princess Margaret at a prestigious trade fair.

On Bank Holiday Monday, 6th May 1985, the Bulls held a champagne party for their friends at the showroom. Nothing at all surprising in that. Patsy Bull was a lively woman, an enthusiastic party-giver and her husband, though rather more reserved, enjoyed a lavish lifestyle. When it was all over, Patsy stayed behind to lock up the shop. There was the usual post-party tidying up to do, but it ought not to have taken her too long and when she failed to arrive home, only 300 yards from the showroom, her son Charles became anxious and went to find out what was keeping her.

Charles found his mother lying on the floor of the storeroom. She was dead and it was obvious that the premises had been ransacked. Little remarkable in that – Coggeshall antiques dealers had been plagued by thieves for several months. But murder? It had never come to that. Charles called the police, who at first were of the view that she had hit her head on the edge of the desk. Had she fallen from a ladder? Had she disturbed the intruders? Had she put up resistance? Had she been killed in a struggle? She was the kind of woman who would have resisted anyone breaking in. Perhaps whoever had come in was after the valuable collection of carved ivory but that seemed intact. Then it was discovered that more than £2,000 was missing from the safe. Only when the body was moved from where it lay was it discovered that she had been shot in the back of the head. A single bullet was embedded in her brain.

Another murder, then, in this telegenic spot. Only two years earlier the doctor's wife, Diane Jones, had been murdered, a case which, at the time of writing, has yet to be solved. It seems so out of place, a murder in Coggeshall, unreal almost, belonging to the realm of fiction, as though happenings such as these in places like this should be reserved for lightweight, Sunday night television dramas.

The police had information about a black car seen in the area shortly before the body was found – a Volkswagen Golf, or a Ford Escort or Fiesta – which reversed into the driveway of the Bulls' house. It had then driven off at speed. The raiders?

A huge crowd turned out for the funeral of this much-liked woman. Her husband sent a wreath of red roses with a note: 'Patsy, I am totally lost without you. Love forever, Wilfred.' But it came from the prison cell in which he had been lodged two days after the murder of his wife. Local people were astounded at this turn of events. Who could believe it? Patsy Bull had been a good wife, hardworking, a woman who had lovingly supported her husband during a leukaemia scare, giving him strength and support at a difficult period. It was impossible to think that he had murdered her. And now Bull was refused bail, despite offering sureties totalling more than £500,000. He was to remain in custody for almost six months, until November 1985, when he was granted bail of £650,000 in part contributed to by friends.

The past came up, inevitably, tales of how 23 years earlier Wilfred Bull had inherited his brother's half of the family business after an accident when they were out pheasant shooting. Not only had Wilfred taken over the business but he had married his brother's fiancée. And now she was dead. But could this man, a loving father and husband, have wilfully murdered his wife? To some in the town it was totally implausible. Others wondered, could he have murdered his brother all those years ago? But no, not Wilfred Bull. Surely not. Absolutely absurd. Two murders? Well, certainly the police were giving the matter some thought.

At the beginning of the five-day trial at the Old Bailey before Mr Justice Jupp in March 1986, William Denny QC for the prosecution warned the jury that Bull was 'remarkably adept' at inventing stories and telling lies. The case was that after murdering his wife, he had told a series of elaborate lies to make her death look like an accident. And the motive? Bull had a lover; his wife had found out and there was the strong likelihood that she would seek a divorce. This would have cost him dear. Would he be able to continue with the business if she insisted on taking half of it? Could he continue with his luxurious life-style if he had to give her half his fortune? Would he lose his mansion, Highlands? 'Divorce,' said the prosecution, 'would have been disastrous. It would have meant dividing everything.' But the alternative was too awful to contemplate because he could not face losing his lover, a widow, Carol Hughes.

In 1984 Patsy Bull had found out about Mrs Hughes whom her husband had been seeing. It was a difficult time. Eventually, after his wife threatened divorce, Bull promised to end the relationship, but he could not keep to his promise to Patsy and continued to meet Carol Hughes in secret. How long matters could have gone on that way cannot be known. It was no flash in the pan romance. It wasn't a short-term fling. Both Wilfred Bull and Carol Hughes were deeply in love with each other. Their affair had already lasted six years. But Bull was determined that a divorce was out of the question.

Wilfred Bull.

And so to the Bank Holiday Monday, the champagne party, and the discovery of Patsy, dead on the storeroom floor. Throughout that afternoon Bull had tried to contact Carol Hughes. He was desperate to meet her that evening but somehow she was unavailable. Time and again he went to the telephone but there was never any reply. On what ought to have been a happy occasion, it was obvious to Patsy that her husband was increasingly miserable and frustrated. She seems to have realized that there was something wrong. Why was he constantly telephoning, she must have asked herself. Was it Carol Hughes he was trying to contact? It was these questions that, according to the prosecution, she put to Wilfred when the guests left. And it was then that she was shot.

Then, after trying to make it appear that there had been a break-in, Bull went across the road to his house. Bull now appears at his most callous and calculating. Within minutes of the shooting, he was on the telephone to a friend. A good day. Yes, a very successful 'do'. And he was planning to take Patsy on a birthday trip, on the Orient Express. She'd enjoy that. No, he told the listener, she couldn't come down, not at the moment. She was 'up to her arms in suds', he said. She was enjoying a bubble bath. But it was all a pretence, that conversation and the hysterical grief when first told of his wife's death. Whilst the police were looking for the car which had allegedly backed into the Bulls' driveway at about the time of the murder, they also searched the house. Their suspicions were aroused by the inconsistency of Bull's story. His wife had been found in the storeroom where, he told his son, he had left her to lock up. So when did she have the bubble bath? Had she come home, taken a bath, and then gone back to lock up? It made little sense.

In a safe under the floorboards in the gun room police found a revolver, a Smith and Wesson, partly covered by gold ingots. Could he explain that? It was the same calibre as the weapon which had been used to shoot his wife. Now Bull's story fell apart. Yes, he admitted, he had killed his wife. But, he said, it had happened accidentally. He kept a loaded gun in the shop for protection against robbers. He had a number of such guns both in the house and the showroom. After all, there had been several robberies in Coggeshall. Antiques shops with valuable contents were always vulnerable.

It was after the party and already the atmosphere was fraught. Patsy's suspicions had been aroused in the course of the afternoon. Now she and Bull were arguing. Bull's version suggests that as they exchanged disagreeable words they were still putting the room straight. He claimed that he had opened the drawer in which he kept the revolver, intending to move it. The gun was wrapped in a pair of tights. Patsy, who had apparently not seen the tights before, had snatched at them. 'Whose are these?' she had asked. In his statement Bull says, 'I was startled and stumbled backwards, losing my balance. The gun went off. I panicked and said, God, what have I done? I just panicked. I didn't know what to do.'

In court, Bull, near collapse, explained how he had accidentally shot his wife. 'I loved my wife,' he said. 'To kill her was the last thing I wanted.' He said that that as she lay dead at his feet, his brother's death had flashed across his mind. They had been out shooting pheasants on Christmas Eve. There was a brick culvert and his brother jumped across it and Bull handed him the gun. His brother suddenly slipped on the ice and fell back. The gun went off and blew off the top of his head. Then, returning to the death of his wife, Bull said, 'The gun went off and she crumpled over. I saw the blood coming from her head and I did not go to her assistance. I could not face reality. I just thought of that tragedy with my brother. I didn't believe it could happen a second time.'

Stunned though he was by what had occurred, he took time to create the impression that the showroom had been broken into. The jury might have found it difficult to accept that a man in shock could be alert enough to construct such a plan. Then he had returned home, telling his son that his mother was locking up. After this he had the telephone conversation, suggesting that Patsy was having a bubble bath.

The prosecution counsel, William Denny, asked, 'How can that callous conversation possibly square with the actions of a supposedly distraught husband who had just accidentally shot his wife?' And, Denny remarked, whilst it was true that Wilfred Bull was seen by his friends as a caring and affectionate father and husband, there was another side to him. 'When in drink, he could be very different and on occasions that resulted in hostility to his wife.'

Charles Bull told the jury how his mother had caught his father together with his lover. He, still a schoolboy, and Patsy had gone to a flat in Chelmsford. His father was there at the time. 'My mother threw Carol to the floor and pulled her hair,' he said. 'I then took my mother away. It was a most unpleasant occasion.' He said that on the day of the murder his mother was worked up, as she thought her husband was seeing Carol again.

Wilfred Bull was found guilty of his wife's murder and given a life sentence. Mr Justice Jupp said he had been convicted on abundant evidence. 'This was clearly murder, although no doubt one done during the course of a quarrel rather than planned.'

There were those who could not accept the judge's observation that it was an unplanned murder. After all, how had Wilfred Bull remained so cool in the hours after the murder? How was it that he had been hysterical when his son told him his mother was dead and yet he had acted normally up to that point? What self-control. On the other hand, had it been premeditated, would not an intelligent man have planned things differently? Would he not have got his stories right? Would he not have ironed out any inconsistencies?

Did it all blow up on the Bank Holiday Monday? Was it the result of a quarrel when Patsy discovered that her husband was meeting his former lover again? Outsiders had thought the marriage unshakeable, but close friends were aware that despite a public pretence of togetherness the couple fought like cat and dog in private. Was the gun suddenly grabbed by Patsy, as Bull said it had been, and did it simply go off? Or was it, as the judge suggested, a murder in the heat of an argument?

After the trial, the police spoke about reopening the case of the brother's death, which at the inquest had been declared accidental. Then the decision was made to abandon the idea. It was all too long ago.

In 1998, when Bull was preparing for release, he was in the news again. He was sentenced to an additional 15 months for trying to sell his collection of 120 white rhino horns. From his prison cell he had masterminded their sale, planning to sell them in the Far East, where they are prized as a medicine and aphrodisiac. Carol Hughes, who had stood by him throughout, and two others, were negotiating on the outside. It was expected that they would sell for about £12,000 a kilogram, which would have netted over £2 million. But the RSPCA had launched an undercover operation and had brought an action against Bull for contravening the 1985 Act which relates to profiting from endangered species. The horns were confiscated. In this matter Carol Hughes was said to have acted out of love and blind trust. Later, on appeal, Bull's additional sentence was expunged and the horns were returned to him. He had not bought them illegally. They had been purchased years before the legislation had been introduced. He was later able to sell about 30 per cent of the original collection.

And finally, where in the hierarchy of villains does a man like Wilfred Bull stand? Pretty low, really. On balance one is inclined to accept that the murder was unplanned. Illicit affairs are not uncommon, nor are rocky marriages, and in such circumstances there are not unexpectedly rows of varying intensity. It may have been an outburst of sudden rage, perhaps drink induced, which led to the shooting. This is not to excuse it or minimise its horror. It simply places Wilfred Bull alongside many other men in his situation whose lives have not quite taken the same awful direction.

BARBARIAN INSIDE
THE GATES

———————— ❁ ————————

Keeping out the barbarians has been the aim of some Frinton-on-Sea residents since first it became an elegant little seaside resort. Why have the rag-tag and bobtail cluttering up the town with their common voices, their whining children, their awful taste in clothes? Why encourage the wrong sorts of residents? Why have all these ghastly modern shops, cheap and trashy? A caricature? Not really. There was, there continues to be in Frinton, some resistance to the onward consumerist egalitarianism of the present age. And particularly 'inside the gates', which, not unlike Oxford's infamous Cutteslowe Walls, mark the boundary between what may be seen as two nations, the old spirit remains. So there are no shellfish stalls or ice-cream vendors, no kiss-me-quick hats or amusement arcades. If you want brashness, noisiness, and tattiness, there are other places on the coast to go to. But under pressure Frinton's inhabitants have more recently accepted, albeit reluctantly, a public house and a fish and chip shop within the boundaries. Otherwise, there is still the whiff of an older, more genteel time and, let it be admitted, of a calmer age. Some seem still to hold to the view that nothing much good comes from a disorderly, undisciplined world 'outside the gates'. Or, put another way, 'from the other side of the tracks', for it is the railway line which cuts the place in two and the railway crossing gates which provide a social dividing line.

Elsewhere in these pages it is remarked that there are towns and villages where even the notion of violence seems outlandish, where it appears to strike a discordant note. And certainly Frinton, undeniably classy and decent, is one of these places. Yet, on 22nd August 1984, the barbarian was within the gates.

In the late afternoon there were two armed raids on local post offices. At 4.30 pm, a man wearing a crash helmet had entered the sub-post office in Walton High Street, where he threatened the staff with a sawn-off shotgun. In less than a minute, he was out of the door and speeding away on a motorcycle, with a haul of several thousand pounds in a plastic bag. Then, only twenty or so minutes later, he was in Frinton where he made a similar attempt at the post office in Connaught Avenue, threatening to shoot a lady customer if his bag was not filled with cash. This time, however, the postmaster gambled and sounded the alarm. The robber ran out and escaped on a motorbike. By the following day, the postmaster might have concluded that he and his customers had had an escape.

The police were quickly on the look-out for the robber. In the last 18 months there had been a series of post office robberies – at Wivenhoe, Bocking, Langford, and Thorington and three in Colchester – and there was some preparedness for another such robbery. Now, at Frinton, road blocks were set up very speedily though the culprit was not found. However, the police had a good description of the man they were seeking from post office staff at Walton and Frinton, and the motorbike was identified as a Kawasaki. One man who appeared to fit the description of the robber was flagged down and questioned by police. They had some doubts as he was riding a Suzuki combination and not a Kawasaki but otherwise he seemed to fit the description of the robber. He claimed to have been visiting his mother at her nearby home. He said that he had been with her all afternoon and, when the man was escorted to the house, she backed up his alibi as did his niece. It was a natural mistake for the police to make. They were anxious to apprehend the armed man and in their enthusiasm they had picked up a wrong suspect. Or so they thought. They were unaware that he had dumped his own motorcycle in his mother's garage and was now riding his niece's machine.

Then the police received an unexpected piece of information. A lady walking along Central Avenue, only a short distance from the seafront, had noticed a man acting oddly. She had seen him dump a plastic bag in some bushes in Peddler's Wood, near the railway embankment. She thought the man was furtive and was concerned that he must be dumping something suspicious. A litter of unwanted kittens, she thought but, though she looked in the bushes for the bag, she could find nothing. Perhaps she wondered if she wasn't being silly, wasting police time when they had such important work to do, but she stifled whatever doubts she might have had and reported what she had seen.

Constable Des Johnson took a call about a litter of kittens or something in the wood. Would he just check on it? He did. The constable met the witness, who pointed out the approximate location of the plastic bag, and he found it. It was clear that there weren't kittens inside. He could see that. Rubbish of some kind, eh? He looked inside. Bundles of notes – £8,705 in cash. He reported in straight away and then took the bag and its contents to his car and replaced them with another bag filled with newspapers, because the owner would be coming back – no doubt about that – and possibly armed – probably armed.

A team of eight police officers of the tactical firearms squad was despatched to Central Avenue. They included Sergeant Brian 'Bill' Bishop, a firearms instructor, and at 6ft 7ins tall, an impressive figure, with 18 years' distinguished service, a veteran of similar dangerous situations. The police took up positions in two teams of four, each in unmarked cars, and lay in wait for the robber. And at half past eight he came, went to where the plastic bag was hidden, and could not find it. He searched and searched, looked here and there, in and out of the bushes, out into the car park. Frantic, panicking, and wondering why it was that he couldn't find the bag, he was sweating and angry; it was absurd. The bag was somewhere, must be. And all the time, the men in Bill Bishop's team were close at hand and had him under close observation. Finally, Bishop opened the car door, eased his huge frame out, and called out to the searcher, the robber, warning him: 'Armed police. Stop.' And then ...

Several days later, Colchester Magistrates Court held a special sitting in a small private room in the Jefferson Ward at Essex County Hospital. A dozen people crowded into the 15ft by 12ft room. In addition to magistrates, solicitors, policemen, a

Sergeant Brian Bishop on duty at Stansted Airport. (Courtesy of Essex Police Museum)

journalist, the governor of Norwich prison and the court clerk, perched on a red-cushioned bench, were the hospital administrator and a nursing sister. In the bed was 35 year old Colin Richards from Brentwood. He was too ill to move but he was conscious and able to hear the charges preferred against him. There were the armed robberies at Walton and the assault with intent to rob at Frinton on 22nd August. There were charges relating to a robbery of the Woolwich Building Society in Chelmsford on 27th August 1982; a robbery at Lloyds Bank, Romford on 1st March 1983, and possession of a firearm at Romford on the same date, with intent to endanger life. His coups, including that in Walton, had brought him a total of more than £18,000.

But there were other charges, infinitely more serious. There were charges of murder and attempted murder, for Richards had turned his fire on the policemen preparing to arrest him.

At his five-day trial in Norwich Crown Court in July 1985, Richards appeared in a wheelchair. He was permanently paralysed from the waist down. The court heard graphic descriptions of what had occurred. Sergeant Bishop's team had decided that it was time to make an arrest. Richards, a black plastic bag cradled to his chest, approached them, unaware of the police presence. Then the sergeant climbed out of the car. It takes no time, any of this, seconds only from Bishop's shout to Richards' response; seconds only for Sergeant Fairweather to stumble, hit by a shot, and then to ease off a round; seconds only for Richards to fall, hit in the back and side, from bullets fired by another of the police team. It takes longer to tell in court.

Bill Bishop had drawn his revolver and called out to Richards, 'Armed police. Stop.' The men were only feet apart. Four policemen, all armed, and Richards. Bishop called out a second time. And then, Sergeant Mervyn Fairweather told the court, Richards 'spun round very quickly and there was a flash and a bang'. He had had his shotgun concealed in the black plastic bag. Bishop fell backwards, wounded in the head. Another shot and Fairweather was hit in the groin. After firing both barrels, Richards had started to fumble with his gun, apparently having trouble with the mechanism. Sergeant Fairweather said, 'I really thought he was going to fire again so I took aim at the centre of his body and fired one shot.' Richards was then challenged twice by Sergeant Brian Waugh. But Richards showed no sign of complying with any order. 'I immediately fired my weapon at the man from a hip position at a distance of about six to eight feet,' Waugh said, and, as Richards then directed his double barrelled shotgun towards him, Waugh fired a second shot. This 'spun him round and dropped him down'. All this inside the gates, in Central Avenue, which leads down to the Leas, the Greensward, the beach, and the sea beyond.

From only a few feet: shots fired in one case from four or five feet away; from six to eight feet in another. Firing at each other from such short distances; Richards taking the risk, deciding to shoot his way out, knowing surely that the chance of someone falling seriously injured or being killed was high. It was the action of a desperate man, a dangerous man, a barbarian inside the gates.

So in seconds Sergeant Bishop, that giant of a man, was crawling, face down, groaning, emitting a kind of whistling sound. He would die five days later from his head wounds. And in only a very few seconds more, Richards would fall, seriously injured, never again able to walk. All this in sight of the sea, in a town which had tried through the years to protect itself from life's coarser, more brutal features.

In the Norwich courtroom, Richards, who denied the charges of murder and attempted murder but admitted the robbery charges, gave his version of events. He had been taken by surprise, and, though he had deliberately fired, he had intended to fire only warning shots. His idea, he said, was that the policemen would take cover, giving him a chance to escape. He had not intended to do more than that. 'Both barrels went off at the same time which took me by surprise,' he said. And Peter Prescott from the Home Office forensic science laboratories acknowledged that Richards' shotgun was faulty. 'If you fire the right-hand barrel the shock will release the mechanism on the left-hand barrel and the left-hand barrel will discharge.' Maybe. But was it a defence? And was it an excuse that he was a business man, that his hardware shop had fallen on hard times, that to save the business he had taken up armed robbery? Could anyone readily feel sympathy for the man whose actions had condemned him to life in a wheelchair? This was no novice gunman. He had belonged to gun clubs. He had, it was later revealed, fired at another policeman when leaving the scene of a previous robbery.

After deliberating for four hours, the jury found Richards guilty of Sergeant Bishop's murder and he was sentenced to life imprisonment. He was found not guilty of attempting to murder Sergeant Fairweather but guilty of wounding him and for this he was sentenced to a further seven years to run concurrently. He was further sentenced to ten years to run concurrently on each of three charges of armed robbery and one charge of attempted robbery and seven years on each of the two offences of using firearms to resist arrest. Passing sentence, Mr Justice Boreham commented that he would have recommended a minimum of 20 years in jail had the injuries to Richards not reduced his danger to society.

This barbarian inside the gates was no hardworking businessman. This was a man who, seeing his business going into decline, had, instead of resolving to repair matters by his own efforts, resorted to violence, attacking a number of post offices and threatening staff and customers. This was a man whose private education had availed him nothing, a man whose mother and niece had given him the alibi that allowed him to go out hours later to murder a man of distinction.

Turning to the courage of all of the policemen involved in the tragic shooting, the judge observed, 'One doesn't need a very vivid imagination to imagine how terrifying it would have been to face that dreadful weapon on that night. I only wish that Sergeant Bishop were here to hear the commendation.'

On the day after the shooting and before Sergeant Bishop's death, Robert Bunyard, the Chief Constable of Essex, called the Home Office guidelines relating to dealing with armed criminals 'dangerous'. 'Our men have not got much of a chance,' he said. 'The rules are dangerous because we are obliged to challenge a gunman and give him a first shot. That is what happened last night.' Days later he enlarged on the problem. 'My men are not trained to disable people who fire at them – they are trained to stop them. But we do not open fire until it is absolutely necessary in order to save life.'

Whenever these occasions occur, the police are on a knife edge and in recent years there have been cases where armed policemen have come under heavy censure for what has appeared to be an immoderate or too hasty use of force.

Even instances which seem clear-cut have raised doubts. In March 1979, Essex Police Support Unit killed an 18-year-old gunman after a countywide chase. He had been cornered in a Harwich pub, where he took prisoners. A siege lasted eight hours, after which the man set fire to the pub, from where he emerged brandishing a shotgun. After a warning, he fired, wounding one policeman in the head. The gunman was shot and killed. A verdict of justifiable homicide was returned at the inquest, but there were still those who quibbled. In these situations the police tread an extremely fine line. They do not make the first move. That is up to their quarry. He has the choice. And, if he decides to shoot, he has an advantage, as he had 'inside the gates' at Frinton, where another courageous policeman fell. The bad news is that the barbarian is always within the gates.

THE LONG
EIGHTEEN HOURS

———————❖———————

It's an ordinary sort of summer evening really. A Thursday. Half past nine or so. James and Edna Andrews are watching television along with 14-year-old James. There's nothing to distinguish today from most of the other days. It's just an ordinary evening in Lexden. They'll watch the programme till ten, or maybe eleven, and then after a last drink they'll be off to bed. It's the way they live. It's the way most people live. Quietly. Orderly. No real highs and lows. And then the doorbell rings. Matthew? – 17-years-old and he still forgets his key. His father goes to the door.

It's not Matthew. There are four of them, and as soon as the door is opened they charge into the hallway. Edna and young James hear the noise, hear the front door slam and the shouts. What's going on?

And now they come into the sitting room, the four of them, with James senior, bewildered, flustered. They are wearing black balaclavas. At least one of them is carrying a shotgun. But the Andrews have nothing worth taking, certainly nothing that would merit a break-in of this kind. There's no jewellery of enormous value, no fine oil paintings, no antiques, and there is no wall safe with wads of notes in it. Perhaps James senior blusters, orders them out. Perhaps young James squares up to them, for at some point the man with the gun hits him in the mouth. It's clear that these men are serious and dangerous. No resistance. They won't have that. They threaten consequences if there's any nonsense, and they're still threatening when Matthew comes home.

And as the initial shock wears off, the family members are able to take in a little more. It's odd, really, but the intruders, all four of them, are smartly dressed in dark designer suits and thin leather gloves. Their clothes are so new looking, as if they'd just come out of some top-class outfitters. And their shoes – funny what you notice in such extreme circumstances – their shiny new shoes still squeak. If it wasn't for the balaclavas, you'd think they were a group of executives just out of the office. But they aren't executives. They are nasty and they're vicious, and they appear to mean what they say. They warn about what they will do if there's any attempt to thwart them. They will castrate the boys and they will rape Edna if anything happens to stop this plan. And then they'll be killed. Understand? So concentrate, they tell James, because the lives of his wife and sons depend on what he does tomorrow. If he cooperates all will be well. But let him slip up, let him call the police and they won't hesitate to carry out their threats.

They all listen to the instructions. The gunman is the boss. He is the one who does most of the talking. He has an accent – German, Dutch, something like that – and he is frightening. Tomorrow, he tells James, he will bring them £80,000 from his place of work. No good James saying it's impossible. No good his saying it can't be done, because 'the German' won't listen to excuses. It will have to be done. Or else.

James, the manager of the Tesco Superstore at Copdock near Ipswich, is told precisely what is expected of him. He'll go to work as normal tomorrow. He'll find the money in the store – he'll have to – and then he'll drive to the Payless car park and leave his car there with the money inside. After that he'll walk to Ipswich railway station. Under no circumstances, he is reminded, must he contact the police until at least one hour after he leaves the money.

Then they are all tied up, blindfolded, and kept for the rest of the night each in a separate room, each with his own fears. 'We were subjected to a night where we were constantly under threat from these people,' Andrews said later. 'We were kept separate and were not aware of the situation with regard to the other members of the family, which was in itself difficult. My wife and children were taken away and I had specific instructions to follow. By not following those instructions, I was left in no doubt as to what the consequences would be – that my family would be killed.

The whole of the next day I was left alone with a decision to make.'

Yes, a decision to make on which the lives of his family depended. The problem was how he was going to be able to get the money. How could he? He was the manager but he didn't have access to money in that way. Big businesses don't have money lying around in fat bundles waiting to be picked up by managers. Yet if he did not find the money, what might happen to the family? And what if he did contact the police? What if they mounted an operation that went wrong? These were ruthless men. He had no doubt that they would carry out what they had promised. He decided that he could not take the risk of calling for help.

In the early hours, sometime after six o'clock, two of the men drove off with Edna Andrews and her sons in the back seat of the family's Fiat Panda. Where to? They had no idea. All three were tightly bound and not allowed to see where they were being taken. What was to become of them?

As instructed, James Andrews drove to the store. How could he get the money? He could not do it on his own – it was impossible – but he'd formulated a plan and he hoped that his colleagues would fall in with it. It was the best he could do. On arriving at work, he called a meeting of his five senior staff and explained what had happened since he last saw them, told them how an apparently ordinary evening had turned into such a nightmare. Would they cooperate? It was life and death. He needed the money by the afternoon. And they understood his predicament. They could not even risk contacting head office because that would only delay matters. It might lead to the police being called. No, they agreed, the solution lay in their hands. They would follow Andrews' plan. In mid-afternoon they would collect all the money from the tills and hand it over as ransom money. And so they did. They collected £55,000 from the tills of the very busy store and at 3.30 pm Andrews drove his Rover into the Payless Do-It-Yourself car park. He left the money in the car. An hour later he contacted the police.

Elsewhere, in a stifling hot car, on an hot summer's day, Edna, Matthew, and James were still tightly bound, uncomfortable, cramped, and wondering what was to happen to them. They wondered if the ransom money had been collected and what 'the German' might have done to James if things had not turned out right. They wondered, too, where exactly they were. Where was this wood to which they had been brought? Since their arrival the car had been camouflaged with nettles and branches. They could see so little.

Then they noticed that without warning the men who had been guarding them were no longer about. They hadn't been to the car windows to peer in at them. They couldn't be heard wandering restlessly about outside, their mobile phone conversations could no longer be heard. They'd gone, just disappeared without a word. Or was it a trick? Well, they could try to get away. It was worth a try. The boys and their mother struggled to release themselves from their bindings and from the locked car. And then they made their way down a lane and eventually found a builder's yard in Needham Market, where they raised the alarm. They were in Suffolk, 20 miles from home. They had been in Baylham Wood for about eight hours.

Shortly after that, James Andrews, at Ipswich railway station, rang the police and learnt that all of his family were safe. Apart from young James who had a bruised mouth, no one had been physically assaulted. But they had all been placed under the most terrifying pressure.

In an investigation covering Essex and Suffolk, the police were speedily into action. They recalled a similarly vicious armed robbery two years earlier, in 1989. A deputy bank manager had been similarly attacked at his home and his family threatened by a gang led by a man with a German accent. He had been forced to go to his bank and take money out of the safe to hand over to the gang. Detective Superintendent Malcolm Hargreaves, who was in charge of the investigation, said, 'This is a very serious offence – it is on a par with a murder inquiry.' He did acknowledge that it had been a very well planned crime but he was confident of success. 'Our track record on such serious cases is very impressive indeed,' he said. 'I would say it was as high as 99 per cent.'

Tesco had offered a reward of £30,000, and the police urged the criminal underworld to turn in the kidnappers, pointing out such a sum was more than anyone in a gang of four would make in a robbery. It was a good incentive for someone to come forward.

Two boys who had been cycling in the area of Baylham Wood at about 3 pm were interviewed about a possible sighting of a gang member who had been guarding Edna Andrews and the boys. On the Saturday James Andrews' missing red Rover was found abandoned in Sainsbury's car park in Tollgate in Colchester. A woman saw a man leaving it and reported this to the police.

Then came a real breakthrough. Despite the gang's immaculate planning, they had made a serious error. They had recruited three small-time crooks to tidy up the evidence and to get rid of the getaway car. When one tried to sell the car radio he raised suspicions and in consequence he and his two companions were arrested within hours. They told police about the man who had employed them, a man known to them as 'the German'.

An appeal on *Crimewatch UK* then led directly to the arrest of the robbers. The gang leader had a theatrical flair which lent itself especially well to the *Crimewatch* formula of dramatic reconstruction. Indeed the thrill of seeing their own exploits turned into the stuff of action-adventure films is said to explain in part the popularity of the programme with criminals. It is apparently compulsive viewing among professional crooks. Much of the programme's most useful information is known to come from the underworld itself. The motivation may be that those who are criminals are disgusted by particular crimes. Or perhaps they are taking revenge. Or eliminating competition. After the *Crimewatch* programme, a flood of calls to the police mentioned a man living in luxury somewhere in London, and more precise information led them to Eltham, to a German. When the police arrived there, however, 'the German' had gone. The following day John Calton was arrested after police in North Wales saw one of his cars parked at a hotel. Two accomplices, Robert More and Sean Wain, both in their early twenties, were arrested later.

After a 25-day trial in 1992, all three accused were found guilty of two robberies and of possessing a sawn-off shotgun. Passing sentence, Judge Peter Greenwood observed, 'It is rare that I have in front of me men who are not only wicked but evil. The vile cruelty you showed when kidnapping ordinary decent people was without mercy and you can expect little from me.' As the verdict was announced, 39-year-old Calton, sitting in the dock, casually

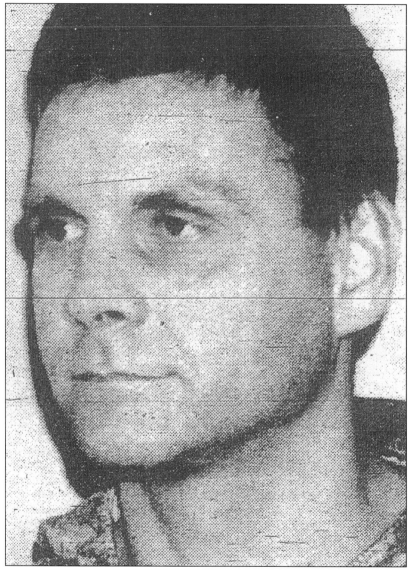

John Calton: 'not only wicked but evil'.

read a horror novel. He was sentenced to 25 years and his two accomplices to 20 years each.

Calton, who had posed at times as Hans Schultze, a German-born motorway engineer, and who used a fake accent on his robberies, was a former paratrooper, a weapons and explosives expert. After leaving the Parachute Regiment, he carried out a series of bank raids in which he claimed to be wired up as a 'human bomb' and terrified bank staff into handing over cash by threatening to blow himself up. In 1983 he was sentenced at the Old Bailey to six years' imprisonment. More recently, Calton and his gang had got away with £96,000 in two violent robberies. In addition to the assault on the Andrews family, the gang had carried out a similar attack on the deputy bank manager of Barclays at Kelvedon. And on another evening in April 1989 they had arrived at the house in Coggeshall where they terrorized Simon Culling, his brother, father and mother. They had been handcuffed and repeatedly threatened with guns.

A former officer in the Parachute Regiment summed up Calton well. He wrote of him: 'He has no regard for human life and would be better suited as a terrorist than a soldier.' That seems to be a fair assessment.

No Escape

---❀---

It's just not the kind of place you'd expect anything like that to happen, not at Thorpe-le-Soken. There are places where the most appalling things occur and you perhaps think to yourself that, well, you're not totally surprised. But Thorpe-le-Soken? Surely not. For a start there's such a sense of openness in this village, such spaciousness, such light and freshness, and the dreadful occurrence in Byng Close was the opposite of all that. It was claustrophobic. It was dark. It was cramped. Airless.

It began with an anonymous call to Scotland Yard from a public phone box in central London. The caller said that there was a dead body in a flat. In Thorpe-le Soken? A hoaxer? Must be. A typical Saturday night call. At 9.15 pm on 18th November, 2000. Somebody with nothing else to do. That's what it must have seemed like, though sometimes neighbours do report unpleasant matters in this way rather than become involved themselves.

In any event, at 10.20 pm, police called at the address they had been given but there was no reply. They left but returned at 4.40 am, and again there was no response. It was 11.45 am when they finally forced the door of the ground floor council flat in Guy Wright House, Byng Close.

There was nothing obvious: no body in the sitting room, nothing in the bedroom or kitchen. But there was a cupboard in the hallway. It was sealed with black tape and had been painted over. They thought they ought to have a look inside, just to check. When they opened the door the smell was overpowering. And inside, in the lower half of the cupboard, was the badly decomposed, half-naked body of a young man. He had presumably died in there and had been left for days, weeks possibly. So small was the space that the body was bent double.

Whoever the man was, he was in a space in which he had had no room to move. A shelf which formed the top part of the cupboard had been deliberately lowered to make the space even narrower. It was only 20 inches wide, $17^1/_2$ inches deep and 30 inches high. It was remarkable that anyone could get into it, but then he was so wasted. Later the body was weighed: four and a half stone. According to the police doctor he had been dead for about three weeks.

They were new people, the neighbours said. They had been there only six weeks or so. And there was such talk and rumours about the four newcomers. Apparently they had moved there from Alvis Avenue in Jaywick and there was a story that there had been an arson attack on their house there. But nobody knew much about them. Even in the cul-de-sac they had hardly spoken to anyone. They were hardly ever seen. And now three of them had disappeared. The fourth was the man in the cupboard, 24-year-old Justin Chant. One of the last people who saw him alive was a midwife who came to visit another of the occupants, Mickala Wrenn. On her way into the house, she had seen Justin and she remembered the large sores on his emaciated body and his skinny, claw-like hands.

The missing woman, Wrenn, only 20-years-old, was pregnant. She came originally from Harold Hill but had not lived there for some years. As a child she had been taken into care. Another of those who had lived in the flat but who could not now be traced was 22-year-old Lee Smith, originally from Clacton. He had an IQ of 73, equivalent to that of an 11-year-old. He had attempted a further education course at Colchester Institute but when young he had had a kidney transplant and now found the travelling to and from college tiring. Poor Lee Smith had made few friends in his life, until he was thrown out of his lodgings in Jaywick and his neighbours asked him to go and live with them. So he met Wrenn. And Justin Chant was there too, living in a shed at the back of the house. And of course there was Stephen Sullivan. He was older than the others, a 40-year-old, quite the master, quite the overlord, the one who told the others what to do, Stephen Sullivan, muscular, menacing. That was the household, the four occupants of the flat in Byng Close.

Within days of the discovery of the body, Lee Smith walked voluntarily into a police station. Sullivan was found by police at the house of Mickala Wrenn's grandfather, and Wrenn too was soon in custody.

At the time of his arrest Sullivan claimed that one morning he had found Justin dead. He had tried to resuscitate him, he said, but was unable to explain why no ambulance was called and the authorities not informed. When Justin's body began to smell the cupboard was taped up and painted over. Sullivan also taped up the door of the nearby airing cupboard, which contained clothes for Wrenn's baby. He did not want them to be contaminated, he told the police.

The police also asked about 30th October when Sullivan, Smith, and Wrenn went to the Crown Court in connection with an alleged arson attack on the Jaywick house. Where was Justin Chant, they were asked. Why had he not attended court? They claimed they did not know. But Justin was already dead.

The trial of Sullivan, Smith and Wrenn at Chelmsford in November–December 2001 revealed a catalogue of cruelty, which Justin Chant suffered for two years, all of it orchestrated by Sullivan. The other two played only minor parts, principally as onlookers, transfixed by the horrors they witnessed and afraid of the ringmaster and his dreadful parade of viciousness.

It may be just bad luck. Maybe if he had lived only half a mile further away, Justin Chant might never have met Sullivan. But they had both lived in Dagenham, just round the corner from each other. Justin lived with his mother and grandmother in a comfortable home. Like Lee Smith, he had few friends. His brother, to whom he was very close, had recently joined the army and Justin missed him deeply. Then Sullivan came on the scene. They met in a video shop, started talking, met again and became friends. Becoming friends was important to Justin. Perhaps because Sullivan was an older man, Justin felt that he was a father figure. Just as Lee Smith felt about him.

But Justin was different from Smith and Wrenn. He had benefited from school, had stayed on until he was 18, was quite good at languages, and was knowledgeable about computers. So how did such a young man fall under the spell of Sullivan? His mother described him as a loving boy. He was quiet and retiring. 'He never went clubbing and did not drink or smoke,' his mother said. 'He was quite happy to stay at home and play on his computer.' His mother never met Sullivan but he had impressed Justin's grandmother as being very nice, like an elder brother, the sort of man who would be a good friend to Justin.

When he was 21 Justin moved to a flat in Barking, and then his mother noticed how he seemed to come to see her or his father only when it suited Sullivan. In the same way, visits to Justin were regulated by Sullivan. But at least his parents could console themselves that he did not take drugs and he still did not drink.

Then came the first of several convictions for petty offences, including shoplifting. After that came a short prison sentence. It was all so out of character. How was it that the young man had changed so radically? The only reasonable conclusion is that he was forced into crime by Sullivan's dominant personality and his own pliable character. It is as if Sullivan had spotted him, picked him out, had known from their first meeting that here was someone he would be able to manipulate, to use as his puppet, his toy to play with. On his release, Justin went to live with Sullivan.

In the two years in which this sensitive, young man lived with Sullivan, he was treated to endless torments, some of them merely mean spirited, others of almost unbelievable depravity. And whilst Sullivan was enjoying himself it must be assumed that Wrenn and Smith, themselves vulnerable but at least not being subjected to such base treatment, stood by helpless.

What occurred first at Jaywick and then at Thorpe-le-Soken all seems so incomprehensible. But not to Sullivan. He had his needs to satisfy. Once he made Justin dig a hole in a field and then he buried him alive. Can you understand this? Can you understand that Justin participated in this task, knowing probably what was to happen to him? Can you understand anyone wishing to inflict such barbaric treatment on another man? If not, you are equally unlikely to be able to understand why, when they lived at Jaywick, there were occasions when Justin was not allowed in the hut that Sullivan had consigned him to and was on several occasions forced to stand outside in the rain. Why did he not run away? Because he was so completely under Sullivan's control.

Then there was the money that Sullivan said Justin owed him. Sullivan would rant about this. What about paying for the damage to the wheel trim of the car? He'd have to pay for that. He'd have to hand over all the money his mother sent him from time to time. And he'd have to pay in other ways. Wouldn't he? So there were the hours Justin spent in the car boot. Once, when Sullivan drove to the DSS office in Clacton, he was placed in the boot at 9 am and stayed there until 10 pm. Imagine it. And he never once tapped hard on the boot lid or shouted out that he wanted to be released. His fear kept him mute.

And use of the bathroom was forbidden. Justin was too dirty to be allowed to use it. He was told that the bathroom was only for clean people, people who looked after themselves. Nor could he use the lavatory. He was provided with a petrol can for his needs. There was the occasion when he was taken to a local campsite where there was a shower room. He was forced to take a cold shower because warm water was forbidden him. When he collapsed with cold he was brought back home and returned to his cupboard. But he had lost one of his trainers. Careless. Needed to be punished for that. Given a rubber glove to wear on his foot. 'Brains', Sullivan called him. Well, 'Brains' has to learn.

This is inhuman. This is the devil's work. Justin has aftershave poured on his hands, which are then set on fire; one of his hands is held over the electric fire until it is burnt; his genitals are burned with a blowtorch; a car battery is clipped to his genitals and the electric charge goes through him. New tortures for Justin. New tortures for Sullivan. In the last three weeks Justin is starved, though sometimes Wrenn dares to sneak him some chips and bread and water and a couple of KitKats. She and Smith have been forbidden to give him food or drink but they cannot now bear his daily anguish. It must be obvious to them all where this is leading. Even to Sullivan. He can if he wishes call a halt to what he is doing. He knows that this is going to end as murder. So why doesn't he stop it? Is it because he cannot? Is it because he is driven on by his inner demons?

Finally, there is the interrogation. It is on video tape dated 26th October, only a day or two before Justin died. He has been brought out of his cupboard, the 'box', as his master calls it, and he stands before Sullivan, his judge and jury. He clutches his hands, his head is bowed, his T-shirt stained, his trousers dirty. It is the pose of a guilty man, of a brainwashed prisoner, of someone who knows he deserves what is coming to him. The voice behind the camera says, 'Hello, my son,' and then asks why he was caught smelling Mickala's knickers.

The penitent answers, 'Because I was jealous.'

(What does that mean?)

Now the interrogator asks how he has damaged his privates. Justin says that someone had put a banger down his trousers.

(Someone? He doesn't say, 'You did it, Sullivan.' No, he cannot accuse father, cannot blame Big Brother.)

Why does he smell, he is asked. Why has he soiled himself? Why are his clothes so dirty? And Justin tries to answer, to explain his condition, accepting that he is to blame for all of this.

Detective Inspector Len Jarman, second in charge of the police investigation, has described this incident as 'an attempt to extract the last little bit of torture out of him'. Justin now had so little time to live and that was obvious to Sullivan. Justin was slipping away from him and before he went he had to be paraded this one last time.

After Sullivan's arrest other victims came forward, out of his past, others who had suffered at his hands over the past 20 years, other vulnerable people who had accepted him as their replacement father and who, almost as if mesmerized, had stayed with him in spite of the most appalling treatment. His stepsister said that she was terrified of him. He had bullied her all his life. Former girlfriends also testified to his cruelty. One said that he had strangled her puppy in front of her. One said that the house they lived in had a torture chamber. This was Stephen Sullivan they were daring to speak of, the natural father of 21 children by 15 different women. And the father-figure to others.

In court, where she appeared on a charge of manslaughter, Wrenn spoke out about the man she had met when she was 16 and he 36, the man whom she had previously never dared to question. She could not stand up to him, she said. He terrified her. He would threaten her for the slightest error. If she as much as looked at other men, he would fly into a rage. He had hit her even when she was pregnant. He bought all her clothes and insisted that she cut her long hair. She could not make choices for herself.

The flat at Guy Wright House was damp, Wrenn said, and Sullivan would complain that his clothes smelled and would order her to wash them. 'I didn't have a washing machine. I did them by hand. Sometimes every day. I had blisters on my hands,' she said. 'There was a tumble dryer but Stephen Sullivan would not let me use it most of the time as it used electricity.' Even at the end of her pregnancy she weighed no more than eight stone because all she was ever allowed to eat was snacks or sandwiches. Sullivan did not approve of her eating anything else except for a curry once a week. He predicted that her child would die. That the baby was born healthy after her arrest might have been a surprise to her. He had said it, hadn't he? Told her the baby would die. And yet it was alive.

So why did she not escape? Because there was no escape. He would find her if she left. After all, she believed that Sullivan had psychic powers. And when he found her what might he do? There was no going away. Ever. And Lee Smith felt the man's power, too, and so they both stayed with Sullivan. Perhaps they were grateful that he had found in Justin Chant someone whom he liked to torture even more than them. Their unquestioning loyalty reserved most of the pain for Justin. It allowed them to share the sitting room with Sullivan while Justin crouched alone in his dark cupboard.

But why did Justin, this relatively intelligent boy, not make his escape? He was different from the others and his trials were more severe. Surely he was aware of how it must all end. Why did this boy who liked languages at school and could cope with computers put up with this life? Because he was so dominated by Sullivan that he had neither the energy nor the will to run away and because in some perverse way he regarded Sullivan as a hero. By the end, he was conditioned to believe that his role in life was to be punished, tortured and humiliated. Perhaps he had some strange idea that he had to obey his master, his harsh father, that he had no choice in the matter. It was what he was there for. And Sullivan went on treating him as no more than an object for his cruelty. The brainwasher and the brainwashed played their complementary parts.

At the end of the six-week trial at which Sullivan declined to go in the witness box, the jury retired for nine hours. Their concern must have related to the responsibility of Wrenn and Lee Smith for there was little doubt of Sullivan's guilt. They reached the conclusion that neither was guilty of manslaughter or false imprisonment. But Sullivan was sentenced to life for the murder of Justin Chant and given a concurrent 18 year sentence for his false imprisonment.

Since the trial Justin Chant's parents have asked for compensation from the Criminal Injuries Compensation Authority. This is established for the benefit of victims of crime. His father and mother have always believed that their son's descent into crime was initiated by Sullivan and his malign influence. They say that until he met Sullivan, Justin led a clean and healthy life. The CICA's rejection of the request is interesting. 'We do not know whether Justin was bullied into committing all of the offences [for which he was convicted] or only some of them, or the degree of coercion applied by Mr Sullivan in each case, or what other factor led to Justin committing the offences.' The statement insists that Justin was responsible for his own actions. 'He was an adult when he committed his offences and was not, as far as I am aware, suffering from any condition that might have affected his ability to understand that he was engaging in criminal acts and what the likely consequences of that were.'

His mother has said that she never suspected what was happening to Justin though she had always been concerned about his friendship with Sullivan. Yet when he telephoned her he always said that he was all right. And then it was all too late.

This is a disturbing case and it is rooted in one man's dominance of others. In human groups there is a small percentage of people who seem to need to dominate. When psychopaths have this urge they will sometimes revert to crimes of an extreme kind. And as the weak and vulnerable become weaker and yet more vulnerable, so the strong and psychopathic become stronger, their offences increasingly vicious and pointless. They inhabit a nightmare world, these people. They live in a world of sadists and victims, a world inhabited at various times by the likes of the Wests, Charles Manson, Brady and Hindley. And Stephen Sullivan.

THE FALL AND FALL OF JIMMY NEALE

---❀---

Jimmy Neale? Talk about having it made. Just let's start by counting his blessings, his advantages. For one thing, he went to a good public school, Pangbourne College, and any boy who takes advantage of such a privilege has a good start in life. Let's not quibble about it, anyway. Let's at least agree that that kind of beginning can be a springboard to a happy, useful and prosperous life.

And Jimmy grows up into a handsome man with considerable charm. That's helpful. Furthermore, it just so happens that he's a brilliant law student who finishes third in the Law Society finals. So, in 1975, by the age of 30 he can set up his legal practice in Head Street in Colchester, his home town, and the firm flourishes. How could it not with such a dynamic and able man at the helm? He has a luxury home, set in five acres of land at Chitts Hill, and a beautiful wife, Rosemary, a former beauty queen and fashion model. They are a glittering couple.

As if that is not enough, he is the highly popular captain of Southgate Hockey Club where he is known as Champagne Jimmy because he keeps a case of champagne in the boot of his Jaguar XJS to celebrate the team's victories. Under Jimmy Neale, the team has many victories as he leads them to three successive European club championships in 1986. Not surprisingly he also wins 42 caps for England and appears in two world cups. He is, of course, vice-captain of Colchester Cricket Club and a good golfer. What else would you expect? That's a good enough start in life, isn't it? Where next? What next for this flamboyant young man about Colchester? The sky's the limit for Jimmy Neale, so it seems.

But the Jimmy Neale story in some degree is not unlike one of the ancient Greek tragedies. These frequently tell of some hero or other, who is right on top of the world and confident of his place there. But the Gods don't like such presumptuousness and so our hero falls. His sin has been his pride, his assumption that he is impregnable. The Gods don't like that at all, they won't have it, and so down falls the great man.

So, away now from Ancient Greece, and off to Colchester in the 1970s, where Jimmy Neale is enjoying life. It isn't that he has offended any Gods, not in Colchester. His sin is that he cannot be satisfied with what he has. There he is, with a wonderful legal practice, a happy marriage, a beautiful home, and a fine reputation. And he throws it all away. He has evidently thought that he can do as he likes, that he is in effect untouchable. That is just not true.

It's hard to credit, almost impossible to comprehend, but this man, so richly endowed, threw it all away. A respected figure, he was found out to be no more than a dodgy lawyer and in 1985 he was struck off for having 'failed to comply with accounts rules and [having] used money for the purposes of other clients'. In other words he had fiddled the books. And it was no twopenny-halfpenny affair. Jimmy Neale was at the centre of what has been described as the biggest law firm collapse.

Leslie Cairns, a car dealer and one of Neale's clients, had come to him with a problem. He was short of ready cash. He needed to buy some top-class cars but lacked the readies. No problem, said Neale. How much did he want? £150,000? Neale would see to it.

He discussed the matter with his partner, Nigel Steed. Could they lend this chap any money? Well, Neale knew that Steed had £250,000 of clients' money on deposit. They could dip into that. There was nothing dishonest about that. It was easy to arrange, and Steed went along with the proposal with the expected condition: that there would be some guarantee that the money would be paid back. No problem, says Neale. There are deeds of a house available as security, he tells Steed.

Unfortunately, Steed was not to know that the deeds of this particular property were already in the hands of Lloyds Bank as guarantee of another of Cairns' accounts. Unaware that he was bankrolling a very fishy car deal, he therefore accepted a forged document and the cash went to Cairns.

Now, just pause a moment. Does Neale not realise that these sorts of crooked dealings often fall apart? He has enough experience and enough nous to recognise the dangers of the kind of dishonesty he is involving himself in. Why does he do it? Because he is sure he can talk his way round anything? Because he has utter and absolute confidence in himself? Because he is trying to prove himself? Because he is irredeemably crooked?

And he doesn't stop here with the initial loan to Cairns. In a law firm there is always money passing through the books. There are house deposits, fees for consultancy and advisory work, a whole range of financial matters. So there is always cash on the move, in and out of many different accounts. Neale presumably thinks that if the arrangement with Cairns gets into trouble, he can dip into one of the other accounts and lend himself the shortfall. And so on, and so on: every time there is a shortfall, he will dip into another account. He's always topping up from one account to another. And in the end Law Society investigators discover that in all there is a total of £1.3 million missing from clients' accounts.

At the Old Bailey trial in January 1985, the court heard how Neale swindled Steed out of nearly £250,000 by putting up false securities to guarantee the loans. He pleaded guilty to six charges of theft, deception and forgery. Sentencing him to three years, Judge John Hazan told Neale, 'What you did in these offences was a disgrace to your profession.' He said he had committed 'a reckless misuse of clients' money on a massive scale'.

The Law Society had to pay a total of £891,000 in compensation to Neale's clients.

Leslie Cairns was sentenced to 18 months' imprisonment for a series of fraud offences valued at £170,000 and involving two Rolls Royces, a Daimler and an Aston Martin.

Neale was obliged to put his luxury home up for sale. Released after serving a year in prison, he found himself persona non grata in Colchester. He was practically destitute and the family existed on Rosemary's earnings from modelling assignments for holiday brochures and selling shoes on an East End market stall. Yet by 1991 he had clawed his way back, running an advertising agency in

Witham. Men like Jimmy Neale are able and confident enough to overcome setbacks that would finish off any possibility of future success for most other people. Once again, he and Rosemary and their three children were living in plush surroundings, at Lexden. There's no stopping Jimmy. Or so you might have thought.

But in the mid-1990s he was in trouble again. In 1994 Neale was before the court on a charge of handling 63 stolen paintings, valued at £2 million. On this occasion he was acquitted but the following year there were charges of a different nature. This time he appeared before Peterborough Crown Court, charged with being involved in a sophisticated conspiracy with Colchester nightclub boss, Frank Aristodimou, to defraud banks and credit companies. Work that Neale was doing for a Peterborough nightclub enabled him to launder proceeds from stolen credit cards through the club's restaurant, entertainment facilities and fashion shows.

The Peterborough Assistant Recorder, Christopher Tickle, said: '... a significant sum was involved. It was a professional fraud. A significant loss was caused to the banks. Of course there was distress to the people whose credit cards were stolen. I regard this as a case of deliberate dishonesty by a man intelligent enough to avoid it.'

His defence counsel claimed that Neale had played only a limited role in the conspiracy, that he had been only a minor member of a corrupt network. 'He was out of his depth in that he was not familiar with the schemes which his confederates in the conspiracy were up to until a much later stage,' counsel explained. 'At that stage he was being cajoled and had some fears that if he didn't co-operate things would go wrong for him. You have here a man who had everything going for him. He was a qualified solicitor in practice and he fell from that position and since then it has been a downhill road for him. He has never really recovered from it.' This defence seems to have been accepted as Neale was sentenced to only 18 months' of which he served nine. The plea that he had been forced into the crime was one which he would come up with less successfully some years later.

In 1997, again down on his luck, having divorced the previous year and now more or less penniless, Jimmy Neale moved to Hong Kong. He secured a job selling Scotch whisky. But – and this is difficult to comprehend – by 1998 he was able to buy a French wine company, which he named JLC Fine Wines Ltd of Happy Valley, Hong Kong. But it was not successful, and the firm amassed massive debts. Neale has claimed that Triad gangs were already interfering in his business. He found himself in debt to the tune of £40,000 to a New Zealander, Michael Bastion, who one day was found dead at the bottom of a five-storey building. There were suspicions that he had been murdered by Macau Triads, to whom Neale was also heavily in debt. Neale told how he had visits from gang members who had threatened him. On one occasion he had had to lock himself in the office lavatory to escape from them. Another time he was manhandled, hooded, and taken to a warehouse where he was told that he must find the money he owed.

As if these anxieties were not enough, in 1999 there was an appalling family tragedy when Jonathan, Neale's son, who for years had been mentally disturbed, murdered his mother. Rosemary Neale was found unconscious in Jonathan's Colchester flat, a halfway house for disturbed young men. She later died of head injuries. In February 2000, Jonathan admitted manslaughter on grounds of diminished responsibility. His mother had been visiting him, he said, and, convinced that she was the devil, he had suddenly attacked her with a rock. Neale attended the funeral, deeply distressed at the loss of a woman whom he had loved.

Then back to Hong Kong he went, still, so he has said, under threats from the Triads. How was he to pay them off? In attempting to do so – and this is Jimmy Neale's tale – he was tempted once more into crime. In December 2000 came his last brush with the law. He was arrested following a successful joint operation by Australian Customs and the Australian Federal Police which led to breakthroughs and arrests in Hong Kong, Singapore, London, and The Hague.

Neale had masterminded the smuggling of drugs into Australia with an estimated street value of more than £6 million. In July 2000, he flew from Hong Kong to France to organise the consignment. Accompanied by Bruce Ridgeway, a Queenslander, Neale visited St Emilion and purchased 940 cases of wine. In 20 of the cases there were concealed 105.5 kilograms of tablets, each containing 50 per cent pure ecstasy from the Netherlands. But there

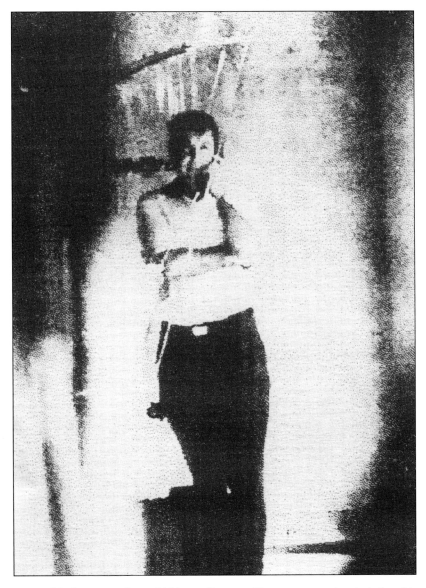

Jimmy Neale captured on a hidden police surveillance camera shortly before his arrest in Australia.

was advance warning to customs and police of what was happening, and the container ship in which the drugs were hidden was shadowed as it travelled from France to Australia. On arrival at the Sydney container terminal harbour, the ship was searched by customs. Using X-ray and particle analysis, they detected the drugs. The tablets were replaced with dummies by Australian Federal Police officers, who then mounted an 11-day surveillance operation.

On 8th December, Neale had 90 cases of wine delivered to a wine store and later he collected two wooden crates containing the dummy tablets. In his hotel room, telephone bugs picked up incriminating conversations with others in Hong Kong and Malaysia, saying that everything was all right and that he had collected the cases. Then Ridgeway turned up and they were overheard discussing the drugs. Hidden video cameras in the room showed Neale removing wine bottles from the crates and taking out the dummy Ecstasy packets. He then put the bottles back, using a towel to wipe them clean of fingerprints. After that, Ridgeway left with the tablets stuffed into a briefcase. The police arrested him outside the hotel. Neale's arrest followed minutes later. At the wine store, about 271,000 ecstasy tablets were seized.

Neale claimed that he had acted under pressure from the Triads. It was a matter of either carry out the smuggling enterprise or die. He said he thought that the 'extras' he was being forced to conceal were viagra and in any case, if it was ecstasy, he disputed the value put on it by customs.

In November 2002, Neale was jailed for life, with no prospect of parole for 21 years. His fellow conspirator, Bruce Ridgeway, was sentenced to 12 years. Judge Penny Hock, describing Neale as 'an intelligent, manipulative and calculating man', said that he was the prime mover in the massive importation of the drugs. She said that 'he recognised he had been caught red-handed and he invented what he regarded as a plausible story in order to try to explain away the compelling evidence against him'. Just as he had done years earlier in the Peterborough case. She said of Neale that he 'has a burning ambition and drive to be part of some financial success story'. And that may be very close to the truth about this complex and deeply flawed man. He has never been satisfied with the success that seems to have attended his life. He has failed to understand that he could have built upon the advantages with which he was born: privilege, ability, charm. He had all of the tools for an outstandingly successful life but was constantly dissatisfied with what he had and therefore followed paths which led each time to disgrace and failure. He wasted his opportunities in the search for ... what? More money? Is that what he was after? Or was it some inner drive to prove himself cleverer than others, confident that he could always evade the consequences if he should fail? It's impossible to say. Perhaps as he serves his life sentence in an Australian prison, he will face up to the truth about himself and what it is that has led him always to the downward slopes. He has time enough because, unless his appeal is successful, he is not due for release until 2021 when he will be in his mid-seventies. What a waste of a promising life.

BIBLIOGRAPHY

———————❀———————

David Bright, *Catching Monsters*, John Blake 2003.
Andrew Jennings, Paul Lashmar and Vyv Simson, *Scotland Yard's Cocaine Connection*, Arrow Books 1991.
Nick Lowes, *White Riot: The Violent Story of Combat 18*, Milo Books 2001
James Morton, *Bent Coppers*, Little, Brown 1993
James Morton, *Gangland 2*, Little, Brown 1994
James Morton, *Supergrasses and Informers*, Little, Brown 1995
James Morton, *East End Gangland*, Warner Books 2001
Bernard O'Mahoney, *Essex Boys*, Mainstream 2000
Martin Short, *Lundy*, Grafton Books 1991
Bert Wickstead, *Gangbuster*, Futura 1985

The author has consulted a wide variety of newspapers and magazines, both local and national. He has also found some useful material on the internet, in particular on the website www.bernardomahoney.co.uk